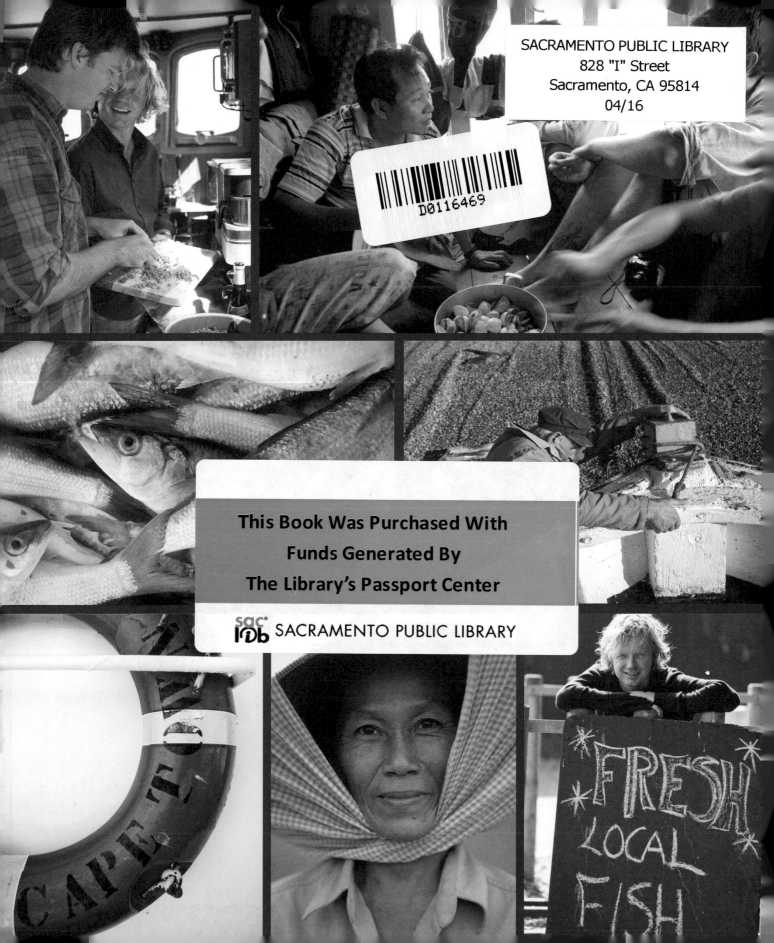

fish tales

fish tales

Stories & recipes from sustainable fisheries
around the world

Bart van Olphen & Tom Kime

Photography by
**Simon Wheeler, Leonard Fäustle,
Chris Arend, & Fred Greaves**

KYLE BOOKS

Published in 2010 by Kyle Books, an imprint of
Kyle Cathie Limited
Distributed by National Book Network
4501 Forbes Blvd., Ste. 200
Lanham, MD 20706
Phone: (800) 462-6420 Fax: (301) 429-5746
custserv@nbnbooks.com

First published in Great Britain in 2009 by
Kyle Cathie Limited

ISBN 978-1-906868-17-8

A Cataloging in Publication record for this title is
available from the Library of Congress.

10 9 8 7 6 5 4 3 2 1

Text copyright © 2009 by Bart van Olphen
and Tom Kime
Design © 2009 by Kyle Cathie Limited
Food photographs © 2009 by Simon Wheeler, except
p77, p176, p179, p182 © 2009 by Leonard Fäustle
Reportage photographs © 2009 by Leonard Fäustle,
except pp10-19 © 2009 by Chris Arend and pp126-
33 by Fred Greaves © 2009 Fishes Holding BV

Design Nicky Collings
Photography Simon Wheeler, Leonard Fäustle,
Chris Arend, and Fred Greaves
Editors Judith Hannam and Vicky Orchard
Copy editor Helena Caldon
Food stylist Polly Webb-Wilson
Props stylist Sue Rowlands
Production Gemma John

Color reproduction by Scanhouse in Malaysia
Printed and bound by C&C Offset Printing Co., Ltd

Bart's dedication
To my mother Annelie for always "being there" and her patience. To
my father Hans for his eternal drive and creative inspiration. To Bo for
bringing me so much joy! To Bernadien for her great love and support.

Tom's dedication
To my wife Kylie Burgess Kime for her continued love, support, and
the exciting future of our family. To my mother Helen for being the
inspiration behind my love of food; to my father Robert for igniting my
love of travel and discovery, and to my sister Hannah for her ongoing
curiosity and encouragement to pursue my goals. To Frank, Alice, and
Raphael my godchildren with whom I look forward to sharing many
meals. To everyone, who loves food and travel this book is for you.

Contents

Disclaimer

At the time of publication the majority of fisheries featured in this book had achieved MSC certification. The Ben Tre clam fishery and Danish mussels fishery were undergoing independent assessment against the MSC standard for well-managed and sustainable fisheries. Certified fisheries undergo an annual review to ensure that they continue to meet the MSC standard, but the easiest way of checking if your fish comes from a certified sustainable fishery is to look for the blue MSC label when purchasing it.

Foreword by the Marine Stewardship Council

The small blue Marine Stewardship Council (MSC) eco-label can be found on the front of thousands of seafood products around the world. Every product featuring the MSC eco-label comes with a promise that the seafood carrying it has come from a certified sustainable fishery. Over one hundred fisheries from all over the world and many, many more seafood companies and retailers are going to great lengths to demonstrate that they catch and supply sustainable seafood... and for good reason: the United Nations' Food and Agriculture Organization reports that over a quarter of the world's fisheries are being overfished or are already depleted, and describes it as a crisis that requires an urgent response on a global level. Where we buy our seafood from and how the fishermen caught it have never been more important. But there is hope. Sustainable and well-managed fishing helps ensure fish stocks are kept at healthy levels and that where ecosystems are damaged or stocks are falling, these will be allowed to recover. The World Wildlife Fund (WWF) recommends buying MSC-labeled products as the first thing we should be doing to help ensure the long-term security of fish stocks.

The science behind the MSC program is formidable. Two standards—one for well-managed sustainable fisheries and another for traceability—underpin it. The fisheries standard took two years to create with input from scientists, governments, environmentalists, and industry experts from around the world. The MSC eco-label is awarded to fisheries that have shown, in an independent assessment, that they do not contribute to overfishing, that they minimize damage to the marine environment, and that they are well-managed. In order to sell products from a certified fishery with the MSC eco-label, each member of the supply chain needs to be certified for traceability. The traceability certification means that fish bearing the MSC eco-label can be traced back to the certified sustainable fishery that caught it.

Fish Tales chronicles the stories of eleven fisheries, some of which have been certified sustainable and others undergoing the MSC certification process. Some are large, like the vast Alaska salmon fishery. Others are small, like the Hastings fisheries fishing from small, beach-launched boats for generations. What all these fisheries share in common is a responsible approach to fisheries management and the aim to achieve or maintain MSC certification, the world's most rigorous independent assessment, to demonstrate they are sustainable and well-managed fisheries.

In many ways, *Fish Tales* is a book about pioneers. Many of these fisheries were the first of their kind to become MSC certified: the first US fishery, the first Norwegian cod fishery, the first African fishery, and so on. Bart van Olphen's company, Fishes, is another of these pioneers. Fishes was the first independent chain of fish shops in Europe to start offering its customers MSC-certified sustainable seafood. While a growing number of retailers now source from a wide range of certified sustainable MSC fisheries, few do it with Bart's enthusiasm.

Demonstrating sustainability helps ensure there will still be fish in the ocean for future generations to enjoy and Tom's recipes remind us what it's all about: the best seafood, sustainably caught and cooked with a passion, is truly wonderful food.

The MSC's vision is clear—we want to see the world's oceans teeming with life, and seafood supplies safeguarded for this and future generations. We are very grateful to Bart and Tom for highlighting the extraordinary work being done by so many people that giving us hope that, as we look forward, our vision can become the new reality.

bart's introduction

My passion for seafood must have developed in the late 70s. I often went traveling with my father and mother through France. The displays of *fruits de mer* left a deep impression on me and I could have spent hours watching the staff opening different varieties of oysters. When I was a kid, I used to go past all kind of restaurants, just to see them operating from the outside.

These experiences inspired me to enroll in a hotel management school. But four years of studying management failed to satisfy me. I wanted to work with the products, so I decided to learn how to cook. I filled a backpack with clothes, the Michelin guide, and a copy of *Escoffier*, and took the train to Paris. I was hired by the first 3-star Michelin restaurant I walked into. I could start the same day, on a salary of zero. After weeks of working in the basement cleaning potatoes and spinach, I started to work upstairs as an apprentice chef. All kinds of artisanal suppliers came into the kitchen. I remember tiny little men arriving every day with fresh catch from Brittany. This was a different world!

I had often thought about starting a fishmonger in Amsterdam as I knew there was room to improve on the service provided by the city's existing fish retailers. I teamed up with one of my best friends, Jesse Keus, and we opened the first Fishes store in Amsterdam just before Christmas 2002. During the early years, we opened more shops. My aim was to offer only high-quality sustainable seafood, but I also wanted to be able to prove to my customers that it came from a really good source. In March 2007, Fishes became the first retailer in continental Europe to be certified by the MSC, but the availability of MSC-certified seafood was modest. Back then, hardly anyone in the fish supply chain really cared about environmental issues. It was very difficult for us to find the right species, sourced from healthy stocks and caught in eco-friendly ways, so I started to travel around to look for possibilities myself. The first fishery we worked with was the Hastings CIC.

After a journey through the elegant Sussex landscape, I disembarked at Hastings. I can remember the sound of the seagulls. Once I spotted the "harbor," I couldn't believe my eyes. The Hastings stade turned out to be a simple platform on the beach, from which only small wooden boats could be launched at high tide. I'd never seen anything like it before. It opened my eyes.

Hastings was the starting point for a quest for sustainable fisheries that has taken me all over the world. I have met down-to-earth, driven people, fishermen at one with nature who instinctively know when they've gone too far. For them, sustainable fishing is just common sense.

Sustainable fish doesn't necessarily taste better than other kinds. A Dover sole with a nice, fat back will always be a beautiful sole. But it's the stories of the people who caught the fish that give it a face. You can pass on the tales in this book during dinner with friends and family, ensuring that more and more people know what's going on. Your number one priority, though, should be enjoying the healthy, delicious fish on your plate. Because that's what it's all about, now and in the future. Enjoy your fish!

tom's introduction

As a boy learning to fish, I was, as the saying goes, taken in "hook, line, and sinker." Starting out, I was spurred on by my mother offering to cook the catch, provided I prepared it. So, aged nine, armed with my pocket knife, I sat outside gutting trout on newspaper, feeding unappetizing bits to my purring cat. As a Piscean and now an avid fisherman, I would much rather prep fish than make a chocolate dessert.

I have traveled widely and found myself in some unusual circumstances in the pursuit of gastronomy. Whenever I can, I use my travels to go fishing, or observe, cook, or eat things fish-related. I marvel at the lively silver fish when they are swimming in the ocean, but I also see it as a delicious part of the next meal. A fish that you release makes you very environmentally aware. How you treat these majestic scaled creatures has a direct impact on the survival of their species. There is no better thrill than fly-fishing for a great fish—and then with one solid flick of the tail it will be off, back to ruling its aquatic domain.

The Latin saying *Piscator non solum piscatur* translates to "A fisherman, not just a catcher of fish"; it is the motto of a tight band of fishing buddies, of which I am a proud member. (Membership of the Serious Waders Club currently stands at six.) We fish in unspoiled places that are barely touched by human activity.

You become a link in a vivid, hungry, aquatic food chain. There is always something bigger down there that has got its eye on the same thing you have. Or is there? The great food chains of the oceans are being assaulted from all sides. These marine habitats are being depleted and damaged beyond repair. Stocks are being swallowed up at a rate that puts their long-term survival in serious jeopardy. Yet our voracious appetite, greed, and lack of knowledge of the deep make it look as if we don't really care, or do not believe the reports that fish supplies in our oceans are running out fast. The advances in aquaculture methods are not addressing the problem that wild stocks are being exhausted.

Sustainability is not a new buzz-word; communities that live by the sea and indigenous people have fished in this manner for millennia. They live by following the seasons, respecting breeding times and aquatic habitats, allowing fish time to mature, and returning juveniles when they are caught. This approach takes a huge pressure off wild species to fight for their own survival. It is only recently that we seem to have forgotten how to respect the natural cycle of life. We must support the oceans so that they can provide us with a bounteous harvest for generations to come.

I want this book to help tell the story of pioneering fisheries around the world. I hope to use my love of food, fish, and far-flung places to educate a broader audience about the importance of harvesting wild fish by sustainable means. I want to invite you to be part of the future of these fisheries and the communities that they support. Ultimately, I want my great-grandchildren to be able to wheel me on to a reef or atoll when I am 98 years old to catch magnificent wild fish in their original oceanic habitat.

alaska salmon & halibut

Species: 5 salmon species have been certified: sockeye
   (*Oncorhynchus nerka*), chum (*Oncorhynchus keta*),
   chinook (*Oncorhynchus tshawytscha*), coho (*Oncorhynchus
   kisutch*), pink (*Oncorhynchus gorbuscha*)
Certification: September 2000; re-certified as of
   November 2007
Location: within US territorial waters adjacent to the coast
   of Alaska

Fishing methods: nets (drift and set gillnets, purse
   seine), trolling, and fishwheels
Fishery tonnage: 287,000 metric tons

Species: halibut (*Hippoglosus stenolepsis*)
Certification: April 2006
Location: Bering Sea, Alaska, Washington
Fishing methods: bottom hook and line (longline)
Fishery tonnage: 24,000 metric tons

alaska salmon & halibut

Emmonak, chum salmon

The Yup'ik Eskimos have been fishing in Emmonak for over 10,000 years. Fishing remains the central economic activity in this tiny city in the Yukon Delta (population 767). During the summer, the salmon industry provides many locals with their only paid work of the year. Just 42 people are kept on after the end of September, but if anything, the importance of fishing to the community increases. It is now a matter of subsistence. Emmonak's remoteness means that food is prohibitively expensive here. Four quarts of milk cost over $50, and Jack, the manager of Kwik'pak fisheries, has just paid $14 for a cucumber and one tomato. Few Yu'pik can afford to shop at these prices, so like their ancestors they must hunt to survive. They pursue moose and ducks on land and seals and whales in the ocean (every fisherman with a boat owns a harpoon). They also continue to fish throughout the winter, this time strictly for their own consumption.

When Kwik'Pak was founded in 2002, the local fishing industry was dying. The establishment of huge modern salmon farms in other parts of the world had caused the price of the fish to drop dramatically over the preceding years, and the logistics of getting Emmonak salmon to market were so costly that it was one of the first places to be abandoned by commercial processors. Kwik'Pak was created to ensure a continued market for locally caught fish and a secure income for Yup'ik fishermen. Today, the firm employs 200 people during the salmon season. It's a real regional effort, encompassing the entire lower Yukon area of about 200 miles of river and delta.

The operation is now running smoothly, with Kwik'Pak supplying chum salmon to customers as far away as Europe. The key to the firm's success is the quality of the fish. The taste is fantastic and the nutritional value is unusually high. Because the Yukon River is so long, the salmon store extra fat for their upriver journey to the spawning grounds. This translates into beautiful red meat with the highest Omega-3 content of any salmon. Yukon chum and king salmon are at least twice and often three or four times as oily as the next most nutritious fish species in America. This makes them among the healthiest fish in the world.

During winter, the Yukon is covered with a layer of ice 5 feet deep. The skiffs that plied the river in summer make way for snowmobiles, but the fishing does not stop. Nets are set through ice-holes in the water to catch local white fish species for the fishermen's own consumption. The Yup'ik also hunt whales and seals, just as they have for millennia.

The locals prefer to cook the fish they catch simply. "Use the whole fish and keep the skin on, on the grill. Add just a bit of seasoning and cook it slowly to keep as much of the juicy oil

top right Fishermen starting their day's work on Kalifornsky beach, Cook Inlet.

bottom right A father-and-son team catching chum salmon on an early night trip on the Yukon River.

"We have lived for 10,000 years in harmony with the land and the seas."

top left A proud young boy with his catch of chum salmon; night fishing on the Yukon River, where it stays light for almost the entire night.

bottom left The local Emmonak bunkhouse.

top right A woman in a typical Yukon fish camp takes care of her homemade smoked salmon.

as possible," advises Robert, chef of the Kwik'pak canteen. This is a cozy little house next to the processing plant where employees come to have their meals in between the hard work. Fish is served twice a week and moose, duck, and other meats are popular as well.

Fishermen in the Yukon Delta do not have total freedom, but they do have a constant and sustainable supply of beautiful fish. This is the result of strict legislation at both state and federal levels. Commercial fishing is confined to two periods. Chum and king salmon are caught from mid-June until the end of July. After a break, the autumn season starts, finishing in September, when the fisherman have turned their attention to coho salmon. This species is less abundant but more lucrative. As local fishermen Alfred explains, "The total annual catch of chum is like 1,000,000 pounds. Coho runs like 350,000 pounds, but the fish pays you double the price."

Alfred and Maxine fish from a steel open Yukon skiff no more than 20 feet long. One skiff houses two fishermen: a captain with a fishing permit and a helper with a license. Alfred's boat was made in a small factory a few villages upriver and differs from the skiffs of hundreds years ago only in the 150 PK Yamaha motor that propels it up the heavy streaming Yukon. The river is lined with mothers with their children fishing by sunset, men alone waiting to take out the fish, and fathers and sons looking on in silence, hoping for a plentiful catch. Women and men do the same jobs on the river. "I was 9 years old when I first went out fishing chum and kings with my father and bought my first permit when I was 14," Maxine relates. "Sometimes it is hard work, especially taking out the nets while the waves are heavy. When you have a good catch it is always balancing the maximum load possible on board. You can easily have the boat full of fish just in one run, but the waves can make you sink."

In the lower Yukon they use drift nets to catch the salmon. Each boat is allowed to carry one net with a maximum length of 160 feet. Fishing, which takes place on a limited number of days per week, starts at 9pm and ends by 6am. After dropping the nets, the fishermen wait for between 30 and 60 minutes before hauling them up again. "It depends on the circumstances," says Alfred. "Heavy wind makes the salmon swim faster." In most cases, the nets are full but it

"I started fishing when I was 9 years old and bought my first permit at the age of 14."
Maxine, fisherwoman, Emmonak

is not rare to haul up a catch of just a few fish. In any case, turnaround is quick. "Normally a skiff comes back one hour after they have left with 2 metric tons of fish and then they will go back again," explains Alfred.

Kenai, sockeye salmon

Cook Inlet stretches 180 miles from Anchorage to the Gulf of Alaska. It is renowned worldwide for the quality of its wild salmon. Sockeye is the main species brought on shore here, but all the Alaskan salmon are fished in these waters. Randy Meier has owned R&J Seafoods, situated on Kalifornsky beach between Kenai and Kasilof, for 13 years. When the season ends, he goes back to the main city of Anchorage to continue his work as a schoolteacher.

The salmon season runs from the end of June until mid-August. In May the beaches are empty, but as the season approaches they fill up with trailers and campers as fishermen take up residence. There is no running water or electricity, but there are plenty of campfires. The fishermen are allowed to catch salmon two days a week, on Mondays and Thursdays, from 7am to 7pm. The boats are an amazing sight as they leave in the early morning. Each one is dragged from the beach into the salty water by three fishermen or fewer. Their long nets have been set within a few miles of the coast to be taken up by the rhythm of the tides. On average, each net yields between 2,500 to 4,000 pounds of fish a day.

Randy owns three boats, each with a permit to set out three nets. The fish are taken out one by one and bled on board to preserve their quality. Slushed ice is then used to bring the temperature quickly down to 34 to 36°F. This is ideal for sockeye, which is the most popular species with the consumer due to its vibrant color. "You cannot go under this temperature as the roe will freeze. The Japanese will not be happy with it," Randy explains.

top left A freshly caught sockeye salmon ready to be taken on board.

top right Fishing for sockeye salmon at Cook Inlet, near Kasilof.

bottom right A recent catch of sockeye salmon at Cook Inlet; fresh sockeye salmon.

"Fishing here is for a lifetime experience, not to make money."

He uses ½ tooths for his fish in order to retain the best quality for the product. A tooth is a small bin used to store the fish on board and the fewer fish stored in each the easier it is to maintain the quality. "Our shelf life is twice that of the Bristol Bay as we only touch the fish when picking," he says proudly.

Randy's main problem is finding good staff. "It's difficult to find the right fishermen," he admits. New recruits are often not aware of how hard the work is, especially when the weather is bad. Taking out full nets of fish during stormy weather is no joke. The fishermen also have plenty to do when they are not at sea, repairing the nets and doing necessary maintenance work on the boats. They can expect to earn a few thousand dollars per season, during which time their housing and food are taken care of by the R&J Company.

top left A young Yup'ik fisherman starts pulling in the drift net, curious about his coming catch.

top right Beautiful fresh sockeye salmon.

bottom right After a full day of catching sockeye, we had a wonderful dinner on the shore with all the fishermen of R&J Seafoods. Fillets of sockeye with just some lime, pepper, and salt were cooked for us on the grill. Delicious!

Everyone loves fishcakes, and these are no exception. In this recipe the large, juicy flakes make a lovely contrast to potatoes that are crushed rather than mashed with chopped fresh herbs, arugula, and cayenne pepper—which give the fishcakes a little kick. They are simple to make and economical, too, as they can be made using leftover fish or potatoes. Serve with a little freshly made mayonnaise.

salmon fishcakes made with herb-crushed potatoes

Serves 4 to 6

10½oz salmon fillets
1½ cups milk
2 sprigs of fresh flat-leaf parsley, stems reserved
10 black peppercorns
2 bay leaves
1lb potatoes, peeled and chopped into even-sized pieces
4 scallions, finely chopped
grated zest of 1 lemon
handful of arugula, coarsely chopped
2 sprigs of fresh dill
salt and freshly ground black pepper
¼ teaspoon cayenne pepper
olive oil, for frying
flour, for dusting

Preheat the oven to 350°F. Place the salmon fillets skin-side down in a roasting pan. Cover with milk, add the parsley stems, black peppercorns, and bay leaves, and cover tightly with tin foil. Poach in the oven for 20 minutes until cooked.

Bring the potatoes to a boil in a pot of salted water. When they are soft, drain and coarsely crush them. You are not making a smooth paste here; you want some texture.

When the potatoes are cool, add the scallions, lemon zest, and arugula. Chop the parsley leaves and the dill together. Add the chopped herbs to the potatoes with salt, pepper, and the cayenne pepper. Mix together, continuing to break up the potatoes without creating a smooth consistency.

When the salmon is cooked, remove from the milk and allow to drain. Flake the salmon and discard any bones or skin. Add the fish to the potato and herb mixture. When mixing together, keep the fish in as large pieces as possible.

Fry a little of the mixture to taste the fishcakes before you roll them all. Adjust the seasoning with salt and black pepper, if desired. Roll the remaining mixture into balls that fit into the palm of your hand or just smaller than a tennis ball. Lightly dust the balls with flour, pat, and then flatten into fishcakes. If the mixture is too wet, add a little extra flour to soak up some of the moisture and hold the fishcakes together.

Heat a pan over medium to high heat. Add a little olive oil and fry the fishcakes until golden brown, about 3 minutes. Using a spatula, gently turn the fishcakes over and brown on the other side. Make sure the oil is hot before you start to cook the fishcakes, and do not overload the pan, as it will cause the temperature in the pan to drop. Drain on paper towels and keep them warm in the oven while you are cook the remaining fishcakes. Serve with roast garlic and herb mayonnaise (see opposite).

This mayonnaise is quick and simple to make and is well worth the effort, providing a decadent finishing touch for the salmon fishcakes.

roast garlic and herb mayonnaise

Serves 6

3 garlic cloves, unpeeled
1 cup extra virgin olive oil
2 egg yolks
1 teaspoon Dijon mustard
pinch of salt
1 teaspoon red wine vinegar
freshly ground black pepper
juice of ½ lemon
sprig of fresh flat-leaf parsley, chopped
sprig of fresh dill, chopped

Place the garlic in a small pan with a little of the oil and cook over medium heat or in the oven at 350°F until golden brown and softened, about 8 to 9 minutes. Set aside to cool. Squeeze the garlic cloves from their skins and crush with the back of a knife. Place the garlic in a bowl and add the egg yolks, mustard, salt, and vinegar. Stir to combine using a wooden spoon.

Gradually pour in the rest of the oil, drip by drip, stirring all the time, to make a mayonnaise. Continue stirring until all the oil is used up and you have a thick emulsion. Add black pepper, the lemon juice, and the chopped herbs and stir to combine. Taste and adjust the seasoning if necessary.

This is a wonderful combination in a very simple recipe. The contrast of textures and the interplay of the colors are as important to the finished dish as the flavors. Everything works together to form a three-dimensional image of delicious food.

grilled salmon with herb lentils and salsa verde

Serves 4

For the herb lentils
7oz Puy lentils
4 fresh sage leaves
3 fresh flat-leaf parsley stems
1 celery rib
salt and freshly ground black pepper
4 tablespoons olive oil
1 tablespoon red wine vinegar
grated zest and juice of 1 lemon
2 sprigs of fresh dill, chopped
3 sprigs of fresh flat-leaf parsley, chopped
3 sprigs of fresh basil, chopped

For the salsa verde
1 garlic clove
2 tablespoons capers, rinsed
1 teaspoon Dijon mustard
3 sprigs of fresh basil
3 sprigs of fresh mint
leaves from 3 sprigs of fresh flat-leaf parsley (stems reserved for the herb lentils)
juice of ½ lemon
1 tablespoon red wine vinegar
3 tablespoons olive oil

oil, for grilling
salmon fillets, 1 portion-sized piece per person, skin on

First make the herb lentils. In a pan, cover the lentils with cold water and bring to a simmer over medium heat. Add the sage leaves, parsley stems, and celery. Simmer until the lentils are *al dente*, and then remove from the heat and drain, reserving a little of the cooking water. Discard the celery and herbs.

Season the lentils while hot with salt and black pepper, and add the oil, vinegar, and the lemon juice and zest, so they will better absorb all the flavors. When the lentils have cooled, add the chopped herbs.

For the salsa verde, place the garlic and capers in a food processor or in a pestle and mortar and blend or crush until smooth. Add the Dijon mustard and all the herbs, then purée until you have a smooth green paste. Add the lemon juice and red wine vinegar, and then stir in the olive oil. Check the seasoning and add more salt, pepper, and lemon juice, if necessary.

Place a lightly oiled, heavy-bottomed griddle pan over medium to high heat. Season the salmon fillets with salt and black pepper and place in the pan, skin-side down. Grill the salmon for 4 minutes until crisp. Roll the fish over and cook for 2 minutes on each of the other sides. When cooking salmon you want the flesh to be medium-rare in the center; the residual heat will continue cooking the fish after it has been removed from the heat.

Serve the grilled fish with the herb lentils and the salsa verde, perhaps alongside some other vegetables or a mixed peppery leaf salad. The richness of the salmon can be complemented by a crisp white wine with a good balance of fruit and acidity. I would suggest a good quality dry rosé.

Making *gravadlax*, by burying salmon in flavored salt (*grave* means bury and *lax* or *lox* means salmon), is a Scandinavian tradition and one of many ways of salting and curing fish. In this recipe, the beets impart not only its sweet, earthy taste—great with salted or smoked fish—but also its highly distinguished and vibrant color. The cured fish is often crusted with fresh herbs such as dill or chopped fennel. Here, toasted coriander and fennel seeds are crushed and scattered over the top. The result is a feast for all the senses. The whole dish looks like an amazing abstract stained-glass window, with a definite wow factor. It takes a bit of time, but is not complicated—and the results are definitely worth it.

beet-cured salmon with dill
crème fraîche

Serves 6 to 8

2¼lb side of salmon, scaled and
    filleted, skin on
2 tablespoons coriander seeds
2 tablespoons fennel seeds
1 teaspoon black peppercorns
4 tablespoons coarse sea salt
3 tablespoons sugar
3 tablespoons vodka
grated zest of 1 lemon
10½oz raw beets, peeled and grated
1 small bunch of fresh dill, coarsely
    chopped
4 sprigs of fresh flat-leaf parsley,
    coarsely chopped

For the dill crème fraîche
1 small bunch of fresh dill,
    chopped
salt and freshly ground black pepper
6½ tablespoons crème fraîche
2 teaspoons Dijon mustard
1 tablespoon red wine vinegar
splash of milk

Place the salmon fillet on a cutting board, skin-side up. Squeeze the sides of the fillet together to tighten the skin and slice away a small piece of skin the size of a coin, leaving a circular nick in the skin to reveal the flesh below. Repeat this three times along the fillet; this allows the juices to run out of the fish while it is salting. Turn the fish over and remove any pin bones with fish tweezers. Line a baking sheet with plastic wrap and place the fish on it, skin-side down.

Coarsely grind 1 tablespoon each of the coriander and fennel seeds with all the peppercorns in a spice grinder or pestle and mortar; you want the spices to have some texture. Combine with the salt, sugar, vodka, lemon zest, and beets, then add half of the dill and all the parsley. Spread the mixture over the salmon and press down. Wrap the plastic wrap around and over the top of the fillet. Place another baking sheet on top and weigh it down with weights, jars, or cans. Leave in the fridge for 8 hours.

Unwrap the fish and wipe off the marinade. Rinse under cold running water to get rid of the salt and grains, then pat it dry with paper towels. Coarsely crush the remaining fennel and coriander seeds and dry-fry them over medium heat for 2 minutes until fragrant. Let cool, then combine with the remaining chopped dill and scatter over the salmon fillet, pressing the herbs and seeds into the flesh. Chill, wrapped in plastic wrap, until ready to serve.

To make the dill crème fraîche, place half the dill in a pestle and mortar with a pinch of salt and pound together to make a green purée. Mix with the crème fraîche, mustard, and vinegar, and season well with salt and black pepper. Stir the remaining dill into the mixture. Add enough milk for a loose consistency.

Cut very thin slices from the fish, starting at the tail end. As you cut them, lay the slices on a piece of wax paper and cover with another sheet. Using a rolling pin, gently tap the slices to get them as thin as possible. Arrange the slices on individual plates and serve splashed with a little of the dill crème fraîche.

This is a simple and very effective dish, both for the eye and the palate. The warm salad and hot-smoked fish are dressed with a thick, punchy sauce, made from watercress, horseradish, and crème fraîche. Salmon, or any other freshwater fish such as trout, works naturally with watercress, and horseradish is also often paired with smoked fish like trout, salmon, or mackerel, because it cuts through the richness of the fish. The sauce works well with roast beef and steak too.

hot-smoked salmon with horseradish, grilled fennel, and watercress salad

Serves 6 to 8

14oz new potatoes, washed
1 white celery heart
2 fennel bulbs
2 tablespoons red wine vinegar
3 tablespoons extra virgin olive oil
salt and freshly ground black pepper
2¼lb side of hot-smoked wild salmon
3 sprigs of fresh flat-leaf parsley
large handful of arugula
leaves from ½ large bunch of fresh
  watercress

For the horseradish and watercress crème fraîche
2 tablespoons hot horseradish, grated
  (fresh or from a jar)
½ large bunch of fresh watercress
2 tablespoons red wine vinegar
juice of ½ lemon
1 teaspoon Dijon mustard
1 cup crème fraîche

Place the potatoes in a pan, cover with cold salted water, and bring to a boil. When the water is boiling, reduce to a simmer.

Meanwhile, pick the pale leaves from the inside of the celery heart and set aside. Finely slice the celery ribs on a diagonal into thin strips. Remove the shoots from the fennel bulbs and reserve any leaves. Cut one fennel in half and trim the root. Finely slice the fennel bulb through the core into thin slivers, which are held together by the central core. Scatter the fennel on a hot griddle pan in small batches and cook until charred in places. Repeat with half the other fennel bulb, then shave the rest and set aside in a bowl of cold water so that it curls up and gets crispy. Mix together the vinegar and olive oil and dress the griddled fennel while hot. Season well with salt and pepper.

Remove the skin from the salmon and gently flake the flesh into as large pieces as possible—it will naturally break up in the salad.

When the potatoes are still firm inside, not falling apart, drain and return to the pan. Add the warm fennel with its dressing and season with salt and pepper. Cover and leave to cool. When just warm, add the chopped celery.

Next, make the horseradish and watercress crème fraîche. Place the horseradish and watercress in a food processor and pulse until you have a coarse green purée. Add the red wine vinegar, lemon juice, and the mustard. Stir in the crème fraîche, and add salt and black pepper to taste. Bring together until you have a smooth, pale green purée. Don't overwork it or the crème fraîche may curdle. Taste the sauce; it needs to be hot, sour, and salty.

Coarsely chop the parsley, reserved celery leaves, and fennel leaves and mix in with the potatoes. Check the seasoning. (Since the potatoes are hot when you season them, they will absorb all the flavors.)

To serve, mix the herbed potatoes with the shaved fennel and the arugula and watercress leaves. Gently mix in the smoked fish. Serve on individual plates or on a large platter. Splash the bright green sauce over the salad.

On a trip to Alaska fishing for salmon, we had an encounter with some bears, who were also looking for a catch. The guides had lit a fire about an hour before and it had broken down to glowing embers, and we decided that the next fish caught would be wrapped up in a parcel and cooked in these embers. We soon had a lovely salmon that had eluded the bears and enjoyed a memorable meal in an extraordinary setting. You can get the same flavor using an outdoor grill or wood fire, or even bake the fish in the oven, but perhaps not replicate the presence of the bears…

whole salmon stuffed with fennel and bay leaves and baked in embers

Serves 6

1 whole salmon, weighing about
   4 to 4½lb, scaled, gutted, and head and
   gills removed
olive oil
salt and freshly ground black pepper
1 bulb fennel, cut into thin slices
1 lemon, cut into thin slices
8 fresh bay leaves
6 large sprigs of fresh rosemary, torn up
4 sprigs of fresh parsley, torn up
½ cup white wine

Light a wood or charcoal fire about 1 hour before you are ready to cook the fish. Build up the fire so that it gets good and hot and burns evenly. If cooking in the oven, preheat the oven to 400°F.

Cut a large piece of heavy-duty tin foil about 4 times the length of the salmon. Fold it so that the length is halved, then fold in half again so that it resembles a salmon-sized book. Take your fish and make sure that the dried bloodline that runs down the inside of its spine is removed with a teaspoon—on a large fish this can be quite substantial and will make the flesh bitter.

Rub some oil inside the fish and on the skin on both sides. Season the fish inside and out with salt and black pepper. Rub a little oil on the left-hand side of the open tin-foil book. Scatter some of the fennel and lemon slices and fresh herbs on the oiled foil. Place the whole fish on top of the herbs and stuff the cavity with more fennel and lemon slices and herbs, scattering the remainder on the top side of the fish. Splash a little olive oil over the top. Seal the long edges and one short edge of the foil envelope. Tightly crimp the edges by folding and twisting them to make a tight seal, which will prevent any juices from leaking out. Pour the wine into the envelope and tightly seal the final short edge.

Spread out the graying embers to make a long space in the middle in which the fish can rest. Position the parcel and move the embers right up close to it, scattering some of the lighter embers over the top. Cook for 12 minutes, then, using a pair of tongs, carefully turn the fish over, being careful not to tear the foil. Re-cover the fish with the embers and cook for another 12 minutes.

Remove the fish parcel from the fire by pushing away all the hot embers. Leave the fish sealed for another 3 to 4 minutes (there will be lot of residual heat inside the envelope) before serving. Carefully cut open a flap in the top of the envelope with a small knife.

You could serve this fish with salad, or if cooking on a fire you could bake potatoes in tin foil in the embers around the fish.

This is a very simple dish to cook; however, it looks striking and the taste definitely leaves you wanting more. I first ate this when I was in Santiago in Chile, where the fish that is most often used is Chilean sea bass. Another suitable deepwater fish from cold waters is halibut, although pollack can also be substituted. In this recipe I have used two fillets of halibut. Use the top and bottom of fillets from the same side of the fish so that they match up, then reassemble them around a filling of fresh herbs before lightly steaming them in portion-sized pieces. They will look like fish and herb sandwiches. To pep up this simply steamed fish, a piquant salsa of green chiles, tomato, oregano, red onion, red wine vinegar, and olive oil is served alongside it. The hot, sour, and salty salsa also works wonderfully with grilled seafood.

steamed halibut with fresh herbs and green salsa

Serves 4

2 medium-sized halibut fillets, skinned
salt and freshly ground black pepper
3 sprigs of fresh tarragon
3 sprigs of fresh flat-leaf parsley
3 sprigs of fresh dill
extra chopped fresh herbs, to garnish
  (optional)

For the green salsa
3 garlic cloves
2 green chiles, such as Serrano or
  jalapeño, seeded and finely chopped
6 medium-sized ripe tomatoes
2 red onions, finely chopped
3 sprigs of fresh cilantro, chopped
½ teaspoon dried oregano
¼ cup olive oil
2 tablespoons red wine vinegar
juice of 1 lemon

Season the halibut fillets with salt and black pepper. Finely chop the herbs and layer them up on the fillets. Put the two fillets back together and season the outside with salt and black pepper.

The fish can be steamed whole as one piece, or it can be cut into portion-sized pieces. Using a sharp knife, slice the stuffed fillets into portions: cut 5 to 6 wedges about 1½in wide, depending on the size of the fish. Cut the fish carefully so that each double piece holds its shape. Wrap the portions in plastic wrap.

Bring some water to a boil in a flat-bottomed steamer. Place the fish in the steamer and cover. Steam for 8 to 10 minutes, or until it is barely opaque.

Meanwhile, make the salsa. Using a pestle and mortar, crush the garlic together with a little salt to form a paste. Add the chiles and continue to pound to make a smooth purée. Transfer the mixture to a serving bowl and prepare the tomatoes. With a small sharp knife, remove the core of each tomato and make a cross in the skin on the underside. Blanch the tomatoes in boiling water for 10 seconds, refresh in iced water, then peel and halve them. Remove the seeds and discard, then finely chop the flesh.

Add the tomatoes and onions to the bowl along with all the remaining ingredients and stir to combine. This vibrant salsa will keep, covered, in the fridge for 2 to 3 days.

Remove the fish portions from the steamer and gently unwrap them, making sure that they do not fall apart. Serve on a large platter garnished with some fresh chopped fresh herbs, if you wish, and with the green salsa alongside. You can also accompany it with a couple of bottles of crisp Chilean Sauvignon Blanc to make it completely authentic.

Here the fish could be served in large wedges that are cut through the bone or in fillets; both look great. The fish is grilled skin-side down so that it is marked and crispy, then roasted in the oven over potato and lemon wedges to lock in all the flavors and juices. The rosemary or bay leaf salt is bright green and highly perfumed, but if you wish you could also add some fennel slices for an extra kick of anise.

grilled and roasted halibut with rosemary, salt, and lemon roasted potatoes

Serves 6

For the preserved lemons
2 lemons
3 heaping tablespoons sea salt
olive oil, for preserving

small bunch of fresh rosemary, coarsely chopped
2 tablespoons coarse sea salt
20 medium-sized potatoes, scrubbed
1 preserved lemon (see above), cut into 12 to 16 wedges
2 tablespoons olive oil, plus extra for cooking
freshly ground black pepper
6 halibut slices on the bone, weighing about 8 to 10oz each
juice of 1 lemon
leaves from 3 sprigs of fresh parsley, coarsely chopped

First make the preserved lemons. Place the lemons in a small pan in which they fit tightly and cover with cold water. Add the sea salt—it takes the bitterness out of the lemon skin. Bring the water to a boil and simmer until the lemons are soft when pierced with the tip of a sharp knife. Remove from the hot water and refresh under cold running water. Transfer the lemons to a sterilized jar (reserve one for this recipe) and cover with olive oil; they will keep, covered, in the fridge for up to 6 weeks.

Preheat the oven to 450°F. Place the rosemary in a pestle and mortar with the salt. Grind until you have a green-colored salt, then remove the stems, leaving a pale green fine salt.

Cut each potato into three even-sized chunks. Mix with the lemon wedges and olive oil and season well with pepper and half of the rosemary salt. Spread the herbed potatoes and lemon mix in one layer in a large roasting pan. Roast for about 35 minutes, turning a few times so that they begin to brown.

Preheat a griddle pan. Oil the fish on both sides and season with pepper and the remaining rosemary salt. When the griddle pan is really hot, grill the fish for 2 minutes on one side until the skin is beginning to crisp. Carefully turn the fish over and cook for another 2 minutes.

Gently remove the fish from the griddle pan and lay it on top of the roasting potatoes. Return the roasting pan to the oven and bake for 10 minutes until the fish is cooked and the potatoes are browned. When the fish is cooked, add the lemon juice and the parsley. You could make some green salsa or another fresh green herb sauce to serve with the fish and potatoes (see page 29).

TIP This flavored salt will keep for about a week in an airtight jar; it is good with roast meat as well as fish and potatoes. You could make a similar salt using fresh bay leaves instead of rosemary.

I first ate this hearty, rustic fish stew in the central fish market in Santiago, Chile. This amazing market is well worth a visit, even if it is just for a bowl of this stew. The nineteenth-century ornate cast-iron quad is brilliantly designed. Around the outside is the fish market with the freshest produce you have ever seen; and the center is full of family-run seafood restaurants, bars, and cafés. From fishmonger's slab to table, via the stove, is only a few feets' distance, and the results are spectacular. The Chileans are renowned for their robust seafood dishes, and this one is traditionally made with *congrio,* or conger eel, but you should use any sustainable firm white-fleshed fish instead, such as halibut, cod, or hake. Like many traditional recipes, it has lots of variations: with or without chiles, potatoes, or cream. Some *caldillo* I tried used tomatoes, while others featured cilantro instead of oregano. The common thread to a *caldillo* is that it is very hearty—your guests will certainly be well-fed.

caldillo de congrio (chilean fish stew)

Serves 6

4 ripe tomatoes
1lb 10oz small potatoes, peeled and
    thinly sliced
2 onions, halved and finely sliced
2 carrots, peeled and finely sliced
olive oil
½ cup dry white wine
salt and freshly ground black pepper
2¼lb halibut fillets, skinned and cut into
    1¼in cubes
4 sprigs of fresh flat-leaf parsley,
    coarsely chopped
4 sprigs of fresh oregano, coarsely
    chopped
4 garlic cloves, finely chopped
2 medium-hot green chiles, seeded
    and finely chopped
1 quart fish stock, hot
juice of 1 lemon, to serve

Preheat the oven to 350°F.

With the tip of a small sharp knife, remove the core from the tomatoes and score the underside with a cross. Bring a pan of water to a boil and blanch the tomatoes for 10 seconds, then transfer to a bowl of iced water. When cool enough to handle, peel them, cut them into quarters, and discard the seeds.

Layer one third of the potatoes in a deep baking dish. Mix the onions with the carrots and scatter half of this mixture over the potatoes with a splash of oil and white wine. Season with salt and black pepper. Lay half the fish on top of the vegetables.

Mix half of the herbs with the tomatoes, garlic, and chiles. Lay half of this mixture on top of the fish and season again. Repeat with layers of one-third of the potatoes and the remaining carrots and onions and fish. Season and add splashes of olive oil and white wine. Add the remaining spiced tomato mixture and top with the rest of the potatoes. Season again with salt and black pepper. Pour the hot fish stock over the top. Place the baking dish over high heat and gently bring to a boil, then bake in the oven for 25 minutes.

Remove from the oven and check that the potatoes are cooked. Serve in large shallow dishes, splashed with a little more olive oil and some lemon juice. Scatter the remaining herbs over the top before serving with lots of crusty white bread, to mop up all the juices, and a very crisp Chilean Sauvignon Blanc.

netherlands plaice

Species: Plaice (*Pleuronectes platessa*)
Certification: June 2009
Location: Central North Sea between Scotland and Denmark
Fishing methods: Twin-rigger trawling, mesh sizes 4½–5½in
Vessels: 4
Number of fisheries: 1

netherlands plaice

Captain Jan De Boer belongs to a huge religious family from Urk in the center of Holland. He is second eldest of 18 siblings. The first mate and engineer are his brothers, and another three brothers are on board the sister ship, the PD143, one of them as skipper. Yet another two brothers run the family business on shore. The bulk of the crew members are between 16 and 22 years old, with the captain's brothers providing some weighty age-earned experience.

12:30am We are on the *Enterprise* PD147 in Thyborøn harbor, North Jutland, Denmark, about to head out for the North Sea between Denmark and northern Scotland.

1:15am Out on the windy foredeck, Albert is coiling huge ropes as thick as my arm. It is his first paid week on board and at 16 he hasn't started shaving yet. If one of those coils springs apart it could knock him unconscious.

1:30am It is a five-hour ride to the fishing grounds. The crew smokes a last cigarette and heads to their bunks for the longest sleep of the trip. Once we arrive, we will be working four hours on, two hours off for 96 hours.

6:30am We are now at the fishing grounds. I am jolted awake by the bell summoning the crew to the nets. It is a beautiful golden morning with a calm sea. The weather forecast is good and I am beginning to recover from my rude awakening. The first of the twin-rigged nets has been launched and they are just about to roll out the second one.

6:45am We stack our boots fire-engine-style with our waterproofs rolled over them. Then we sit patiently at the table looking at our breakfast while we wait for the Captain. Solemn prayers are followed by a rapid meal of bread, cheese, ham, and black coffee.

7:15am There is plenty of laughter as the crew smokes a few cigarettes each, then they head back for another power nap before the nets come in. That's when the real work will start.

The family firm Seatopia is a premium seafood brand supplying fish to businesses all over Europe. Traditionally, fishing boats in the North Sea go out for five to seven days on end, which means that the catch can be ten days old by the time it arrives at a restaurant table. The *Enterprise* returns to harbor every 48 hours, whereupon the crew unloads the catch and puts it on a truck bound for the Netherlands and on to the rest of Europe. Seatopia delivers premium seafood "from ship to shop" within 72 hours of catching it. "The fish that you are catching is always top-quality. The difference is in the transport. When you are able to deliver the fish from the catch to the plate within 72 hours, then you get five-star-plus quality." The crew members fish for five consecutive days, driving over 600 miles in seven or eight hours to get to Urk by

top right Thyborøn harbor, North Jutland, Denmark. Hard work is part of all aspects of this trip, even before we head out into the North Sea.

bottom right The twin-rigged nets are launched to catch plaice. The crew are either working, or eating and sleeping. There is no in-between and no television on board.

"My father was also a very lucky fisherman. We like working very hard."

top left The bell has sounded and the nets are about to be brought up with the catch of the last four hours. For the team on the cutting tables this is the signal for five or six hours of relentless work against a river of live fish.

bottom left The bulging catch of sustainable MSC-certified plaice wait in the nets to be processed.

top right A brief moment of sitting down on the job shows that these tough, hard-working fishermen are still really boys who appreciate the small pleasures in life.

early Saturday morning, then leaving at midnight on Sunday to return to the *Enterprise*. The boat is in operation 48 weeks a year. The crew work five or six weeks on, with one week off. They also take breaks at Christmas, Easter, and other Christian festivals.

In order to be certified as sustainable by the MSC, Seatopia had to change its fishing methods and dramatically rebuild its boats. In 2006, the company's two boats' beam trawlers were converted into twin-riggers. Beam trawling involves a lot of hard work for very little profit. "As a beam trawler we fished 48 weeks a year for 550 metric tons of plaice," says Jan. "Now we do 550 tons in five to six months." The changes to the boats had a drastic effect on the quantity of fuel consumed. The 5,000 horsepower engines were removed and replaced with 2,000 hp models. This reduced weekly diesel consumption from 60 to 20 tons. With fuel priced at around $4.00 a gallon, this has made quite a difference. The company has also benefited from an increase in the landing price of their fish as a result of MSC certification. "Now we spend $15–22,000 with a top landing price of $100,000."

10:45am The alarm goes off again. The crew scrambles into their orange pants and head out to nets that are already being winched in, much to the delight of dozens of raucous seagulls.

11:00am The bulging nets have been hauled aboard, emptied and reset. A thick stream of live fish of all shapes and sizes stretches from the back of the boat to the preparation areas along a continuously moving belt.

11:05am – 2:05pm I used to do all the fish prep at Rick Stein's Seafood Restaurant in Padstow, England, but I have never seen speed like this. These boys move like lightning, gutting and sorting the marine harvest that comes toward us in an unbroken river.

2:05 – 3:05pm The gutted fish are tossed into a raised central channel between the two cutting benches and are then carried away to be sorted and boxed by size. It all happens so quickly you can scarcely see the thick-gloved fingers move.

4.05pm My heart sinks. I was pretty sure that the flow of fish was thinning and the end was

"Fishermen and environmentalists should learn together."

in sight. Then the alarm sounded and the gutting crew of which I am now a part looked up to see the next net hauled over the side of the *Enterprise*. In no time the catch is released to slither its way toward us and we didn't even get to the end of the last batch!

5:05pm It has been all hands on deck for the last two hours and all the fish is finally prepped—for now! Stepping down from the tables, I am utterly exhausted. I have been on the line for six hours, gutting a couple of tons of fish without really moving my feet.

5:30pm After washing and prayers, I try to mimic the stance of the young fisherman as they eat. They hunch over their bowls so that their forks have little space to move between rim and mouth. The captain says that I look as though I have never seen food before. It feels like he has a point. I have always had huge respect for the produce that I cook with, but this experience has taken it to a new level.

Jan is confident that "in time the fish will sell itself." The top five fishmongers in the Netherlands are highly enthusiastic about Seatopia's plaice. Among those singing its praises is Bart van Olphen of Fishes, whose aim is "to support the fishery and educate the consumer." Seatopia, for its part, is eager to show other fishermen the possibilities provided by sustainable fishing and MSC certification. "Now it is as if the fishing boat has been put in a stadium. All eyes are on the fishermen and there are no secrets any more." The fishing industry has rightly been under increasing pressure from consumers, governments, and non-government organizations (NGOs) like Greenpeace. To complement its MSC certification, Seatopia has decided to put webcams on top of its boats to make the whole process completely transparent. Consumers can now see for themselves exactly how the fish is caught and prepared. Within the MSC's chain of custody, a ticket is put on each fish when it is caught and boxed. It still bears this label in the supermarket, showing exactly where and when it was caught and by which boat. Seatopia has been certified only since June 2009 but Jan is already seeing the new approach bear dividends: "We are the first, like a snow plow, but many other fishermen are thinking about how they can change. The consumer is already paying 30–40 percent more for the MSC label. Now that they see that we get a better price, there is action."

top left The refueling time after work and prayers and before sleep. Meals are generally quite silent on board the *Enterprise* as the crew is exhausted.

top right Seatopia's promise of five-star quality fish from the catch to the plate within 72 hours starts its journey.

bottom right While the nets are dry and on deck, the crew is not making a wage, so speedy repairs are carried out so that they can be put back in the water as soon as possible. The vivid almost luminous markings of North Sea plaice. The markings on each fish are as unique as a fingerprint, and for a real connoisseur, they can pin point the fish to a particular region of the North Sea.

The food from the small island of Penang, which borders Malaysia and Thailand, has been very influential on the larger region as a whole. The cuisine is famous for its great seafood dishes and its almost compulsory use of fiery red chiles. The hawker stalls and street food of Singapore, Malaysia, Penang, and Thailand are legendary and evoke scented memories for anyone visiting this region. We tried a bounty of different dishes and local seafood specialities, but a flat fish grilled like this at a night market in Penang was definitely the favorite. Writing this recipe brings back great memories of this vibrant island—if you love good seafood, take a trip to Penang.

grilled marinated penang fish with chile, garlic, and ginger with lemongrass and black pepper dressing

Serves 4 to 6

5 red chiles, seeded and finely chopped (use less if you prefer it less spicy)
3 garlic cloves, finely chopped
1 large piece of fresh ginger, peeled and finely chopped
4 sprigs of fresh cilantro, finely chopped
1 tablespoon fish sauce
juice of 1 lime
2 large plaice, weighing about 18oz each, gutted

For the dressing
4 lemongrass stems, finely chopped
pinch of salt
1 teaspoon sugar
2 garlic cloves, finely chopped
4 sprigs of fresh cilantro
2 teaspoons freshly ground black pepper
1 tablespoon fish sauce
juice of 2 limes
2 tablespoons water

In a pestle and mortar, grind together the chiles and the garlic. (Add a little salt to work as an abrasive and help break down the fibrous spices.) Add the ginger and cilantro and work into a paste. Add the fish sauce, the lime juice, and a splash of water.

Take the cleaned fish and cut four diagonal slashes in the skin on each side, right down to the bone. Make the cuts from left to right and then repeat with another four cuts that will form diamond-shaped markings in the flesh. (These cuts work in three ways: first they allow the spice-packed paste to permeate the flesh; second they allow direct heat to penetrate right to the bone, caramelizing the flesh and creating a great flavor; third they allow easy access for your guests to remove the roasted flesh, leaving nothing but bare bones on a cleaned platter.) Rub the chile paste into the slashes on both sides of the fish. Leave to marinate for 10 to 20 minutes.

Meanwhile, preheat the broiler or an outdoor grill and make the dressing. Place the lemongrass in a pestle and mortar with the salt and sugar and pound to make a coarse paste. Add the garlic, cilantro, and black pepper and continue to pound until you have a semi-smooth paste. Add the fish sauce, lime juice, and water and mix until well blended.

If cooking on an outdoor grill, you will need a thin metal grid rack, such as a cake rack. If cooking under the broiler, you will need a flat baking sheet lined with tin foil. Arrange the plaice according to the chosen method of cooking and cook for about 7 minutes (or shorter depending on the heat of your broiler).

When the fish is cooked, transfer to a large platter, drizzle the lemongrass and black pepper dressing over the top, then watch the fish be devoured in a matter of minutes.

This is a spring and early summer dish with a wonderful combination of vegetables and fresh herbs in varying shades of green. The key to success with this recipe is to dress the vegetables when they are hot; they will absorb all the flavors of the lemony dressing and herbs and the taste will be transformed. The dish will look striking with all the different textures against the simple cooked fish.

grilled fillet of plaice with a salad of asparagus, fennel, and fava beans

Serves 4 to 6

2 fennel bulbs
bunch of asparagus
olive oil
salt and freshly ground black pepper
10½oz fava beans, shelled
   (frozen are fine)
juice of 1 lemon
1 tablespoon red wine vinegar
1 plaice fillet per person, skin on
3 sprigs of fresh mint
3 sprigs of fresh basil
handful of arugula

Preheat a large grill pan with a metal handle that can go into the oven. Slice the fennel in half through the root, remove the tough outside layer, and trim the heart but leave it intact so that it holds the bulb together. Slice each half into six thin slices, cutting to the heart each time so that the small fan shape is held together at the bottom.

Take the asparagus and snap each one wherever the stem naturally breaks. The part toward the spear will be the most tender; discard the tough base. Lay the asparagus flat so that they are all pointing the same way. Slice the stems into three even lengths diagonally, so they resemble penne pasta.

Place the fennel slices and the asparagus pieces in a bowl, add a splash of olive oil, and season with salt and black pepper. When the grill pan is hot, sear the fennel slices and then the asparagus for 2 minutes each side.

Meanwhile, bring a pan of salted water to a boil. Cook the fava beans until *al dente*, about 2–3 minutes, then drain. Mix together the grilled fennel, asparagus, and beans. Season with salt and pepper and add 3 tablespoons of olive oil, the lemon juice, and vinegar.

Preheat the oven to 400°F. Keep the pan hot after you have cooked the vegetables in order to cook the fish. Rub the skin side of the fillets with a little oil and season with salt and pepper. Lightly oil the grill pan. Place the fish skin-side down in the pan and cook for 2 minutes, then carefully lift the fish, rotate it slightly, and replace it on the same side on the pan. Cook for another 2 minutes, then transfer the whole pan to the oven. Bake the fish for 4 minutes.

Coarsely chop the mint, basil, and arugula and mix them with the cooled vegetables. Check the seasoning again and serve warm or cold with the grilled fish fillets. Spoon the olive oil dressing over the fish. If you like, you could add some crispy cooked strips of pancetta to the vegetable mixture for additional texture and flavor.

In this Moroccan-style recipe, whole fillets of plaice are cooked in a tagine with aromatic spices including *ras al hanut,* which is blend containing turmeric, nutmeg, and many other spices. Translated as "head of the shop," *ras al hanut* was traditionally made to a secret recipe created by the spice merchants. There are numerous variations that may include as many as 27 different spices and aromatics, among them delicate rose petals, but in this recipe I have used a simple blend that is easy for you to make at home.

spiced fish tagine with cumin, cilantro, and cayenne pepper

Serves 4 to 6

For the *ras al hanut* Moroccan spice blend
2 teaspoons ground cinnamon
1 teaspoon ground turmeric
1 teaspoon coriander seeds
½ teaspoon freshly ground black pepper
¼ teaspoon freshly grated nutmeg
¼ teaspoon ground cardamom
¼ teaspoon ground cloves

olive oil
2 garlic cloves, finely chopped
3 onions, finely sliced
1 teaspoon cumin seeds
2 teaspoons freshly ground *ras al hanut*
(Moroccan spice blend, see above)
½ teaspoon cayenne pepper
3 ripe tomatoes, seeded and coarsely chopped
salt and freshly ground black pepper
⅓ cup fish stock or water
1 plaice fillet per person, skinned
juice of 1 lemon
4 sprigs of fresh cilantro, roughly chopped

Place all the ingredients for the *ras al hanut* in a pestle and mortar or an electric coffee grinder (see tip below), grind to a fine powder, and set aside.

Place a flameproof terracotta tagine over medium to high heat. If you do not have a tagine, use a shallow saucepan with a tight-fitting lid or a baking dish. Add a little oil and cook the garlic until pale golden and fragrant. Add the onions and reduce the heat. Cook the onions for 8 minutes until softened.

Push the cooked onion to one side of the tagine or pan and turn up the heat a little. In the space that you have created, add the cumin seeds, the *ras al hanut*, and the cayenne pepper and cook for 2 minutes or until fragrant and aromatic, then stir them into the onion mixture.

Add the tomatoes and season with salt and black pepper. Cook for 1 minute to combine the flavors. Add the fish stock or water and bring to a simmer. Taste the mixture and adjust the seasoning if necessary.

Add the whole fish fillets to the tagine or pan and spoon the tomato mixture over the top. Cover with a tight-fitting lid, turn the heat down to low, and cook for 8 minutes. The beauty of a tagine is that it can be brought to the table as part of the table setting. If you do not have a tagine, you could start the onion spice mixture off in a pan, then transfer it to a shallow terracotta dish with a lid and bake the fish in the oven. Bake at 350°F for 12 minutes.

When the fish is ready, remove the lid, squeeze the lemon juice over the top, and scatter with cilantro. Serve immediately with rice, couscous, or potatoes.

TIP For best results when making the *ras al hanut*, buy a small electric coffee grinder that you use only for grinding spices. Once you've mixed all the ingredients, store the blend in an airtight jar. It will keep indefinitely, but it will lose its pungency over time.

This dish combines great flavors and colors; its appearance on the plate is impressive but it is deceptively simple to prepare. The white fish looks sensational against the red and green dressing, the olive tapenade, and yellow olive oil. The tapenade could be made with green or black olives or a combination of the two, and can be made in advance because it will keep in a sealed container in the fridge for a couple of weeks. It is also delicious served with other cooked fish or meat dishes and salads or pasta.

roast fillet of plaice with roasted tomato and basil dressing and green olive tapenade

Serves 4

olive oil
2 garlic cloves, finely chopped
1 small onion, finely chopped
4 sprigs of fresh basil, stems chopped
    and leaves reserved for the dressing
⅓ cup white wine
1 (14oz) can chopped tomatoes
¾ cup fish stock
salt and freshly ground black pepper
pinch of sugar (optional)
4 plaice fillets, skin on
16 cherry tomatoes, halved
1 garlic clove
juice of ½ lemon

For the olive tapenade
pinch crushed red pepper flakes
4 tablespoons green olives, pitted
juice of 1 lemon
4 tablespoons extra virgin olive oil

Place a medium-sized, heavy-bottomed pot over medium heat. Add 1 tablespoon of olive oil, the garlic, and onion and gently cook for 5 minutes, without letting the onion brown. Add the basil stems and cook for another minute. Add the white wine and simmer to allow the alcohol to evaporate and the wine to reduce by half.

Add the chopped tomatoes and the fish stock. Turn down the heat and allow the sauce to simmer for 15 minutes. Break the tomatoes down with a wooden spoon. Taste and adjust the seasoning with salt, black pepper, and a little sugar, if necessary.

Meanwhile, make the tapenade. This olive paste can be completely smooth when made in a food processor, or more textured if cut by hand—whichever you prefer. Crush the pepper flakes together with a little salt until smooth. Coarsely chop the olives, then chop, pound, or blend them until you have your preferred texture. Add the chile, lemon juice, and olive oil. Taste and adjust the seasoning. Season the mixture well with pepper (the olives are salty).

Preheat the oven to 400°F. Score the skin side of the plaice with 3 cuts that cut into the flesh. Pat the fish dry with paper towels and season with salt and pepper. Heat a splash of olive oil in a heavy-bottomed frying pan over medium to high heat. Place the fish in the pan, skin-side down, and cook it until it is a medium golden brown. Do not move the fish, poke it, or shake the pan to allow it to form a brown crust. Gently turn the fish over and cook on the flesh side for 2 minutes. Transfer the fish to a roasting pan with the halved cherry tomatoes and bake in the oven for 5 minutes.

While the fish is baking, make the basil dressing. Crush the garlic with a little salt in a pestle and mortar. Coarsely chop the reserved basil leaves, add them to the pestle and mortar, and quickly pound to make a smooth green paste. Add the lemon juice and 5 tablespoons of olive oil.

When the fish is cooked, plate it up with the roast cherry tomatoes and serve with the hot tomato sauce, the basil dressing, and the tapenade.

vietnam clams

Species: clam (*Meretric Iyrata*)
Certification: Currently under assessment (September 2009)
Location: Ben Tre province, Binh Dai district, the Mekong Delta,
   South Vietnam
Fishing methods: by hand or metal rakes with a net pocket
Fishery tonnage: 4,000 to 6,000 metric tons
Vessels: fished on the strong low tides of the lunar cycle, which
   exposes the clams

vietnam clams

Twice a month, at the middle and the end of the moon's cycle, the vast sand flats of the Mekong Delta in South Vietnam are exposed by strong lunar tides. For five days around each of these deep tidal pulls, the delta yields up its bounty of clams. No machines are allowed for the harvest. Instead, the clams are cut by hand in the same way they have been for centuries. To view this fishery was an extraordinary privilege and a journey back in time.

The fishery, whose name Rang Dong means "the rising of the moon," is one of three cooperatives in the Thoi Thuan commune. It owns ten farms that harvest clams for the market. The Ben Tre People's Committee Department of Fisheries has been working closely with the WWF Community Fisheries Program to achieve environmental acknowledgement from the Marine Stewardship Council. This collaboration between the WWF and the Vietnamese provincial government has resulted in the possibility that the Ben Tre clam fishery will become the first MSC-certified fishery in Southeast Asia. The price of clams has already increased by 30 percent at landing, and new markets have developed as word about possible certification has spread. Keith Symington, Marine Program Coordinator at WWF Vietnam, and Meredith Lopuch, Director of the Community Fisheries Program at WWF United States, are proud that "Ben Tre could be a successful MSC certification of a small-scale fishery in a developing country." The WWF is now working with other communes in the region eager to be certified as sustainable so as to not be left behind. They would like the whole province to become certified, and believe this would "help Vietnam secure its future, when trading with Europe and elsewhere, giving them preferred supplier status."

There are about 1,000 farmers who collect clams for the Ben Tre cooperative when the tides are lowest. During the bi-monthly harvest there are around 300 locals per day on the sand flats, working in family or small community groups. For the rest of the month they work for themselves, catching fish and growing fruit and vegetables for market. In the hot season between January and April when there is no rain, the farmers make salt.

Throughout this area of the southern Mekong you are never more than a few yards from water. Farms and smallholdings perch precariously on the banks of waterways and irrigation ditches. Rivers and freshwater pools hold ducks, frogs, and fish both wild and farmed. Tidal estuaries and saltwater pools are used to raise crabs, sea fish, and large shrimp. There are also salt evaporation pens. Throw in the coconut palms and many types of fruits grown in the region and you have a very lush tropical scene. In an area with such a long coastline and large

top right Ominous monsoon clouds highlight the sand flats of the Mekong Delta. Clams are cut from the exposed beds when the moon's pull creates particularly strong tides.

bottom right Workers of the Ben Tre fishery heave sacks of graded clams on to the waiting wooden boats. With the high tide, the painted craft transports the harvest to the factory to be cleaned.

"Before the cooperative was started in 1975 in Ben Tre province, they used to harvest everything. Now they choose the biggest clams, returning the rest to mature."

top left Freshly cut clams are brought to other members of the village to be sorted. Everyone works together for the benefit of the community.

bottom left Despite the arduous work on the sand flats, the air was filled with laughter and good humor. Everything was shared, including the ride home.

top right The natural bounty is graded by hand while villagers catch up on the latest gossip and local news. Any undersized clams are left where they drop to be redistributed by the rising tide.

river deltas, everything that swims or lives near water is revered in the kitchen. To spend some time in this rural community in the depths of the Mekong delta is bliss. It is such a relief to be out of the constant traffic and noise of the big city. After a local lunch of stir-fried frogs, spiced fishcakes, and a big bowl of sour fish and vegetable soup, we are hurried back on to the waiting scooters. Yet despite the apparent urgency, we are pointed to two hammocks and told that "we must have a siesta! To wait for the tide…"

Riding on a scooter behind one of the Rang Dong officials reveals the remoteness of our location. The off-road journey takes us on top of steep-sided drainage ditches and tidal canals, where we dodge dogs, chickens, children, and other scooters ferrying workers along the rocky paths to the clam beds. We dismount and roll up our pant legs to start the next stage of the expedition. This involves traversing about a ½ mile of thick oozing mud and a number of fast-flowing inlets to the firmer sand flats that lie exposed by the retreating tide.

When describing Ben Tre as a community fishery, I really do mean that the whole community is represented. The youngest Vietnamese worker I saw digging for clams was about twelve, while the oldest lady sorting the shellfish must have been in her eighties. Three hundred members of one community were represented, working hard to dig, sort, grade, wash, and transport the gleaming white clams. Some groups worked in near silence while others shared local gossip and village news. It was a perfect example of each working for the benefit of all.

The pace across the clam beds was brisk, with runners and porters of all ages shifting heavy sacks from one stage in the sorting process to another. At one point I saw a bicycle being pushed through the shallow water. About ten minutes later, the bike was being pushed in from the other side of the tidal clam beds laden with eight 80-pound sacks. The wind had started blowing and the bike was being steered by one man and pushed by a couple of helpers. The full

"This is a good model for how one fishery can pave the way."

sacks were then hauled on to one of a handful of wooden boats that were beached on the sand, waiting for the deep lunar tides to run back in and float off the harvest.

We were called from the sand like hungry children being summoned to the table. Climbing aboard one of the brilliantly painted boats, we were served a pan of clams as fresh as such a dish could possibly be. The steaming shellfish were transferred straight from sand bed to pan and then from stove to bowl in a matter of minutes. Vietnamese cuisine is fragrant, aromatic, and perfumed as a result of the large selection of raw herbs that are torn and eaten with the food. A bowl of mint, Thai basil, and cilantro was served with the freshly steamed clams. It was the perfect thing to dip them all into. The herbs were accompanied by a small dish of roasted salt and crushed black pepper, together with some wedges of lime. Roasting the salt in a dry pan gives it a smoked, nutty flavor. The addition of the lime juice produces a hot, sour, and salty dip for the sweet clams and fragrant herbs. The combination was absolutely spectacular.

As delicious as this impromptu meal was, nothing could have prepared us for the feast of shellfish that was about to be cooked in our honor. We ate 15 different clam dishes over the next three days. Eight of these delights were served in one sitting. It is hard to know where to start when each dish was so unique and delicious. We had clams simply steamed with a

above An impromptu meal on the roof of one of the painted Mekong boats had everyone licking their fingers. The sweet clams and the bright red chile dipping sauce were slurped up in minutes.

"By creating a community cooperative, the members are 80 percent better off than when they fished individually."

above With the winds of the monsoon racing across the shallow water, the transportation of the heavy sacks of clams gets more difficult.

fiery red Vietnamese dipping sauce of chile, garlic, and ginger with fish sauce and lime juice, a combination of flavors so addictive that the pan was emptied in no time at all. We had clams with lemongrass and black pepper, clams steamed with young bamboo, and a delicious hot and sour clam soup, which is one of the specialities of the region. There was also a spectacular dish of fried clam fritters in which the raw meat was dipped into a thick batter of coconut cream and rice flour and then fried until golden and crispy. These were very popular around the table. When we could not eat any more, a platter of grilled clams in the half shell was served with a fiery paste of green chile and scallions.

It is still impossible to choose my favorite clam dish of this visit. There were many dishes that I had not tried before but all will be remembered. What was most special, however, was the respect the harvesters had for the clams. Everyone we met in the district loved eating them and wanted to share their community's recipes with us. These delicious bivalves are much more than a livelihood for these people. They are the very stuff of life and rightly a source of intense local pride.

The sweetness of clams and the ease of cooking them makes them a favorite in any coastal region, where their freshness can be assured. This is a very simple recipe to prepare, consisting of only a few ingredients, and the flavors are delicious. There is no polite way of eating this sort of dish—you just need to dive in! You could use mussels instead of clams, or a combination of the two.

stir-fried clams with thai basil and chile jam

Serves 4

2 lemongrass stalks, tough outer
   leaves removed
2¼lb clams
2 tablespoons oil
1¼in piece of ginger, peeled and cut
   into matchsticks
3 tablespoons Thai chile jam (see below)
⅓ cup water
1 small bunch of fresh Thai basil,
   coarsely chopped
1 small bunch of fresh cilantro,
   coarsely chopped
1 tablespoon soy sauce
juice of 2 limes
freshly ground black pepper

Finely slice the lemongrass stems. Wash and clean the clams thoroughly, then soak as described on page 60. Discard any shellfish that do not close when tapped, are broken, or smell.

Heat a heavy-bottomed pan or a wok over medium to high heat. Add the oil and cook half the ginger and lemongrass for 1 to 2 minutes until fragrant and aromatic. Add the chile jam and the clams. Cook over high heat, stirring to coat the clams with the jam. Add the water, cover with a lid, and cook for another 3 minutes, shaking the pan occasionally. Remove the lid and stir from the bottom. Cook for another 2 minutes until all the clams have opened.

Add half the Thai basil and cilantro, and all the soy sauce and the lime juice. Season with plenty of black pepper. Taste and adjust the seasoning if necessary. Serve in bowls with all the juice. Garnish with the remaining herbs, lemongrass, and shredded ginger.

There are many different versions of chile (*prik* in Thai) relishes, pastes, and jams, where the ingredients are either roasted, cooked separately, or cooked down in a pan together to form these delicious condiments. Make a large batch and store in sterilized jars as you would jam or chutney, or buy some in Asian supermarkets and gourmet food stores.

thai chile jam

½ bunch of cilantro stems and
   roots, finely chopped
2 medium-sized onions,
   coarsely chopped
4 garlic cloves, finely chopped
6 large red chiles, seeded and finely
   chopped
2in piece of ginger, peeled and
   finely chopped
3 tablespoons vegetable oil

Preheat the oven to 400°F. Place the cilantro in a bowl with the onions, garlic, chiles, ginger, and half the oil, and combine. Spread this mixture out on a baking sheet and roast in the oven for 15 minutes until the onion starts to caramelize. Remove the baking sheet from the oven and scrape the contents into a pestle and mortar or food processor. Add the brown sugar and a little salt and blend to a rough paste.

Cut the tomatoes in half. With a cheese grater, grate the flesh side of the tomato, holding the skin side in the palm of your hand. The skin will stay in the flat of your palm.

2 tablespoons soft brown sugar
salt and freshly ground black pepper
3 ripe tomatoes
2 tablespoons tamarind pulp
2 tablespoons fish sauce
⅓ cup water
juice of 1 lime

Heat the remaining oil in a heavy-bottomed pan over medium heat. Transfer the paste to the pan. Add the tamarind pulp, tomato pulp, and the fish sauce and water. Lower the heat and cook for 25 to 30 minutes until the excess liquid has cooked away. Add the lime juice and mix together. Taste and adjust the seasoning. It will keep for about 3 weeks in the fridge or can be stored in sterilized jars like a chutney or relish.

To sterilize jars: before filling, wash them and their lids, tongs, etc. with hot, soapy water. The jars should be made of glass and free of any chips or cracks. Rinse well and arrange the jars and lids open-sides up, without touching, on a baking sheet. Place in a preheated 225°F oven for 25 minutes. Or, boil the jars and lids in a large saucepan, covered with water, for 15 minutes. It is said that a quick hot wash in the dishwasher also works, but I still do it the old-fashioned way. Use tongs when handling the hot sterilized jars, and be sure the tongs are sterilized too by dipping the ends in boiling water before use for a few minutes. Place the hot contents into the hot jars and seal the lids while everything is hot to create a vacuum. Use a dry kitchen towel to handle the jars so that you do not burn yourself. Allow to cool naturally. Do not open the jars before you are ready to serve the contents, as you will break the seal.

The sweetness of small clams is truly amazing when they are cooked quickly and simply. They need a bit of cleaning to avoid a gritty sauce, but not much more preparation. They cook in minutes and are one of my favorite seafoods; they encourage you to roll up your sleeves, tuck a napkin into your shirt, and dive in. If you visit the coastal regions of Italy, you will find a variation of this wonderfully simple dish. As with many dishes from around the world, the key to success is getting the best ingredients you can. Use good white wine—if you wouldn't want to drink it, why bother cooking with it? You need lots of really fresh clams, good olive oil, fresh parsley and garlic, and juicy lemons.

spaghetti vongole
with garlic and parsley

Serves 4 to 6

6¾lb clams
4 tablespoons extra virgin olive oil
3 garlic cloves, finely chopped
2 red chiles, seeded and finely
   chopped
⅓ cup dry white wine
large bunch of fresh flat-leaf parsley,
   coarsely chopped
grated zest and juice of 1 lemon
salt and freshly ground black pepper
14oz spaghetti or linguine

To clean the clams, place them under cold running water for a few minutes, then leave them soaking in fresh water for about 10 minutes. Go through each clam separately, cleaning off any barnacles, and then tap each one to see that it closes. If does not close, throw it away as it is already dead, and discard any that are broken or that smell, too. Be vigilant with shellfish: just one that is off can turn the rest bad and ruin the meal for you and your guests. Leave the good clams soaking in clean, fresh water for another 30 minutes, then drain.

Heat half the olive oil in a heavy saucepan over medium to high heat. Add the garlic and half the chiles and cook for 1 minute until they start to color and smell aromatic. Add the clams and the white wine. Cover with a lid and cook over high heat for 3 minutes. Shake the pan and stir the clams from the bottom a couple of times during cooking to distribute the heat.

Remove the clams with a slotted spoon and reserve the cooking liquid, straining it through a fine sieve lined with cheesecloth or muslin to get rid of any grit (there is nothing worse than a gritty pasta sauce). Clean the saucepan and return the strained liquid to the clean pan. Remove half of the clams from their shells and discard the shells. Throw away any clams that have not opened while cooking.

Bring the strained liquid back to a boil and add the remaining chiles, lemon juice and zest, and chopped parsley. Taste the liquid before seasoning—it will probably be quite salty from the clams.

Meanwhile, bring a large pan of salted water to a boil and cook the spaghetti or linguine until it is *al dente*, about 7 minutes. Strain the pasta and return it to the pan with the remaining olive oil. Mix together and season with freshly ground black pepper. Add all the clams, shelled and unshelled, to the hot sauce. Stir in the pasta; mix thoroughly so that all the noodles are covered in the sauce. Serve immediately.

There are many variations of hot and sour soup throughout Thailand, Vietnam, and Southeast Asia as a whole. The main tastes are hot and sour; however, salty and sweet elements are also present and vital to the balance of the whole dish. I had a wonderful hot and sour fisherman's soup in a village in the Mekong Delta in southern Vietnam; there the sourness came from fresh slices of unripe baby pineapple. The freshness and acidity produced an amazing result.

hot and sour soup of mussels and clams
with caramelized shallots and thai basil

Serves 4 to 6

For the stock
1 tablespoon vegetable oil
2 lemongrass stalks, crushed with the back of knife
5 slices of fresh ginger
4 shallots, coarsely chopped
5 garlic cloves, coarsely crushed
3 red chiles, seeded and coarsely chopped
4 fresh cilantro roots, coarsely chopped
1 quart chicken or fish stock
4 kaffir lime leaves, torn
3 tablespoons tamarind paste
2 tablespoons fish sauce

For the soup
vegetable oil, for cooking
6 shallots, finely chopped
2 teaspoons soft brown sugar
2¼lb mussels, cleaned and scrubbed
2¼lb clams, cleaned and scrubbed
juice of 4 limes
2 tablespoons fish sauce
1½in piece of fresh ginger, peeled and cut into matchsticks
2 scallions, finely sliced
3 sprigs of fresh Thai basil leaves, coarsely chopped
½ medium-sized bunch of fresh cilantro, coarsely chopped

First make the stock. Heat the oil in a heavy-bottomed pan and add the lemongrass, ginger, shallots, and garlic. Cook over medium heat until golden brown. Add the chiles and cilantro roots and cook for 2 minutes until fragrant and aromatic. Add the stock, the lime leaves, and half of the tamarind paste. Add the fish sauce and simmer for 20 minutes.

Meanwhile, start the soup. Heat a little oil in another pan over medium heat, add the shallots and the sugar, and cook until caramelized and golden, about 10 minutes.

When the stock has been simmering for 20 minutes, add the mussels and clams. Cover the pan and cook over medium to high heat for 5 minutes to open the shellfish. Stir the clams and mussels from the bottom to make sure they are all cooked and open. Discard any that remain closed.

Strain the liquid through a large colander, saving all the juice. Remove the shells from about two-thirds of the shellfish. Discard all the chopped vegetables and spices. Clean the pan, then strain the liquid through a fine sieve lined with a piece of cheesecloth or muslin back into the pan.

Add the juice of 3 of the limes, the fish sauce, and the remaining tamarind pulp to get a really good sour flavor. Taste it: the soup should be hot with chile, sour from the lime and tamarind, salty from the fish sauce. Add more of anything if necessary.

Bring the soup back to a boil and return all the shellfish to the pan. Arrange the serving bowls in a line. (It is as easy to serve 4 or 20 bowls with this method, if you want to cook a larger batch to feed a crowd.) In the bottom of each bowl put a pinch of shredded ginger and scallion and a spoonful of caramelized shallots. Add some mussels and clams, then pour the soup over the top. Garnish each bowl with some chopped basil and cilantro and a squeeze of lime and serve. Stir from the bottom of each bowl and dig in.

While visiting the clam fishery in the Mekong Delta for this book, we were generously fed many different dishes of the local clams. In total, fifteen different recipes of clams were cooked for us. All of them were delicious, exciting, vibrant, and very memorable. I think, however that, the most striking and intoxicating was the very simplest. This dish was cooked for us on a wooden boat beached on the sand. We sat on the roof of the fishing boat cross-legged and dug into these clams. They were served in the pan with the vibrant dipping sauce in a bowl beside it. The thought of this dish immediately transports me to the wonders of South Vietnam.

simple steamed clams with a vietnamese red chile dipping sauce

Serves 4 to 6

4½lb clams
⅓ cup water
2 sprigs of fresh cilantro
2 sprigs of fresh Thai basil
salt and freshly ground black pepper

For the red chile dipping sauce
¼ cup water
2 teaspoons rice vinegar
1 teaspoon sugar
2 red chiles, seeded and finely chopped
1 garlic clove, finely chopped
¾in piece of ginger, peeled and finely chopped
juice of 2 limes
2 tablespoons fish sauce

First prepare the clams. Wash and clean them thoroughly, then soak, as described on page 60, discarding any that are broken, open, or smell.

For the dipping sauce, bring the water to a boil with the vinegar and sugar. Boil for 1 minute to melt the sugar and then allow to cool. Mix with the chiles, garlic, ginger, and the lime juice. Stir in the fish sauce.

For the clams, heat a large high-sided saucepan over high heat. Add the water and when it is hot add the cilantro, Thai basil, and clams and lightly season with salt and freshly ground black pepper. Cover and cook over high heat for 4 minutes until the clams have began to open. Vigorously shake the pan a couple of times and stir the clams from the bottom so that they cook evenly. Leave the pan covered and remove from the heat.

In Vietnam they do not cook the clams until they have completely opened, but only until they are just beginning to yield. This means that the clam contains much of its juice still in the shell. Having been shown this method, I was eager to adopt it for this dish as clams cooked this way are definitely the most delicious. Discard any that are still tightly closed, however.

Serve the clams in a large bowl or even in the pan, depending on the occasion. Nothing else is needed except the dipping sauce alongside. The sauce is hot, sour, and salty and the clams are deliciously sweet. I adore food like this— perfection, with as few ingredients as possible. The taste sensation of the clams with this sauce will hopefully knock your socks off.

When I was seven, my family went on vacation to Block Island in Rhode Island. I can still remember the delicious clam chowder that we used to have for lunch; even now I could describe to you exactly how it tasted. This is a classic New England-style clam chowder that is flavored with bacon and thyme and thickened with potatoes and cream. When making a dish like this, it is really important to have the best-quality and freshest ingredients in their simplest form. Make lots of this hearty chowder because everyone will want seconds at one point or another.

clam chowder

Serves 6

6¾lb clams
¾ cup water
olive oil, for cooking
3½ smoked bacon or pancetta, cut into
  ½in dice
2 tablespoons unsalted butter
2 garlic cloves, finely chopped
2 large onions, cut into ½in dice
2 celery ribs, cut into ½in dice
2 bay leaves
3 sprigs of fresh thyme
2¼lb potatoes, peeled and cut into
  ½in dice
¾ cup good-quality heavy cream
salt and freshly ground black pepper
juice of 1 lemon
3 sprigs of fresh flat-leaf parsley,
  coarsely chopped, to garnish

Discard any clams that are open, broken, or that smell. Wash and clean the others thoroughly, then soak as described on page 60. Add clean water to a large high-sided pan and bring to a boil. Add the clams and cover with a tight-fitting lid. Steam for 4 to 5 minutes, shaking the pan a couple times so the clams cook evenly. Stir the clams up from the bottom, replace the lid, and continue to cook for another 3 minutes. Remove the clams from the heat and strain the liquid into a bowl through a fine sieve lined with muslin. Discard any that remain closed.

Remove all the clams from their shells. Place in a bowl and refrigerate until ready to use. The clams will be firmer after this time and easier to cut up. When the clams are cool, cut them into ½in dice.

Heat a heavy-bottomed pan over medium to high heat (you could use the same pan that you cooked the clams in, as long as it is rinsed out). Add a splash of oil and the diced bacon. Cook over medium heat to release the fat and allow the bacon to crisp. Drain off the fat, reserving half the bacon and 1 tablespoon of oil in the pan; set the rest of the bacon aside for the garnish.

Sauté the butter, garlic, onions, and celery in the hot pan. Add the bay leaves and the thyme. Cook gently for 10 minutes until the vegetables are softened. Add the potatoes and enough clam broth just to cover them. Bring to a boil, cover, then turn down the heat and simmer for 10 minutes until the potatoes are cooked. Once the potatoes are softened, crush some of them against the side of the pan so that they release their starch and thicken the soup.

Take the pan off the heat and add the diced clams and the heavy cream. Season with lots of black pepper and the lemon juice; you may not need salt, as the bacon and the clam liquid are salty. Remove about a third of the soup and blend in a food processor. Return this to the pan to thicken the chowder.

Set aside for 30 to 60 minutes to allow the flavors to meld. When ready to serve, reheat the chowder over low heat—do not let it boil. Spoon into bowls and garnish with the reserved bacon and the parsley.

This is a vibrantly robust dish that requires you to roll up your sleeves. The sweet characteristics of the clams and the beans will always work with salty pancetta, bacon, or, in this case, chorizo sausage. The heat from the chorizo and the dried chile adds another dimension to this sweetness. The addition of the unique dry sourness of the Fino sherry makes this dish a match made in heaven.

baked clams with white beans and chorizo

Serves 4 to 6

3½oz dried cannellini beans
2 garlic cloves, crushed
1 celery rib
4 sprigs of fresh flat-leaf parsley, stems and leaves separated
1 sprig of fresh thyme
4 tablespoons olive oil
1 tomato, halved
2 chorizo sausages, cut in half lengthwise, then into thin slices
1 onion, finely chopped
1 small dried chile, crushed
salt and freshly ground black pepper
4½lb clams
2 tablespoons of red wine vinegar
squeeze of lemon juice (optional)
⅓ cup Fino sherry or dry white wine

Soak the cannellini beans in a bowl of water overnight. The next day, preheat the oven to 350°F. Drain the beans, transfer them to a high-sided roasting pan and cover with 1¼in water. Add the garlic, celery, parsley stems, and thyme with 2 tablespoons of the olive oil and the tomato halves. Cover the pan tightly with tin foil. Place the roasting pan on a burner over high heat for 5 minutes until the water begins to boil. Transfer the pan to the oven for 1 hour.

Meanwhile, prepare the other ingredients. Heat a large, heavy-bottomed, ovenproof pan over medium to high heat. When it is hot, add a splash of oil and cook the chorizo for 5 minutes until caramelized. Drain off the excess oil, then add the onion and the chile. Season well, reduce the heat, and cook for another 5 minutes.

Next, prepare the clams. Discard any that are open, broken, or that smell. Wash and clean thoroughly, then soak, as described on page 60.

After 1 hour, remove the beans from the oven. Remove the tin foil carefully, as there will be a lot of trapped steam that will come out as a jet. Check to see if the beans are soft. If not, re-cover and return to the oven; if they are, pour off most of the liquid, leaving just a few spoonfuls to keep them moist.

When the beans are done, turn up the oven temperature to 400°F. Remove the tomatoes from the bean mix using a slotted spoon and chop into a pulp, discarding the skin. Return the tomatoes to the beans and mix in a little oil, all the vinegar, and the chorizo and onion mixture. Taste and adjust the seasoning, adding a squeeze of lemon juice. The flavor of the onions, beans, and chorizo should be sweet, salty, sour, and hot. The beans will stay warm until needed, or if you wish to prepare them in advance, they can be warmed up before serving.

Heat the pan in which the chorizo was cooked over high heat and add the remaining oil. Add the clams and sherry or white wine and mix together. Spoon in the beans, chorizo, and liquid. Bake for about 5 minutes in the oven until all the shellfish have opened. Discard any that do not. Coarsely chop the parsley leaves and scatter over the cooked shellfish. Spoon into large soup bowls and serve with lots of crusty bread to soak up all the hot juices.

denmark mussels

Species: wild-caught blue-shelled mussels (*Mytilus edulis*)
Certification: Currently under assessment (September 2009)
Location: Limfjord in the north of Jutland in Denmark
Fishing methods: small-scale dredging at depths over 10 feet
Fishery tonnage: 40,000 metric tons
Vessels: 90 x 30 foot fishing boats can fish the fjord. All the boats are
  privately owned. The license holder of each boat must be a fisherman.

denmark mussels

Limfjord, in the north of Denmark, is famous for the quality of its oysters and mussels. The cold water means that the mussels gain weight more slowly than their relatives in warmer European seas. This gives the meat a better, firmer texture and a sweeter taste. The people of the region have been fishing mussels from the pristine waters of the Limfjord for centuries. The shellfish themselves have been in the fjord for much longer—fossilized mussels have been found in the area dating from 55 million years ago.

The small town of Nykøbing is situated on the island of Mors in the Limfjord and boasts the largest of the ten harbors around the fjord. The town is painted in bold colors and the small mussel boats in the old harbor are equally vibrant. They are painted red, blue, and green with bright white and pale blue trimming. Many of the hulls are made of copper, which repels algae and other would-be adherent species. It also means that there is no need to paint them, which is a major environmental plus as boat paint is generally considered to be highly toxic. Practicality aside, the tarnished copper hulls look wonderful as reflections of the harbor play across them. These boats look like they were the models for the children's variety found in the tub.

Nykøbing is also home to the Vilsund fishery, the largest of three fisheries on the fjord. Its company claim is that "the Limfjord is nothing less than the world's best mussel and oyster water. This is a wild fishery that naturally produces its stock," the Vilsund publicity material continues. "What we are doing here is fishing for wild mussels rather than farming or manipulating them in any way." The only additional method that is used to boost the productivity of the fishery is relaying undersized seed mussels in better-quality water. In areas of the fjord where there is thick mud or rotting vegetation on the seabed, there are often lots of small shellfish that cannot grow because of the lack of oxygen. Dredging the mussel seeds and relaying them in better-oxygenated water allows them to thrive. Any mussels found to be less than 2in long during the first stage of processing are also relaid in suitable areas of the Limfjord.

Vilsund is the visionary creation of Paul Kergol, whose family has been fishing mussels for generations. The business once concentrated on cleaning mussels for export, but this changed with the tragic drowning of Paul's father and brother. Paul inherited the company at the tender age of 15 and with the help of his mother transformed it into a cooked-mussel business. This allowed Vilsund to operate year round. Now 43, Paul has built the firm into the region's biggest fishery. He is also the proud owner of three boats. He runs the business in a very hands-on manner, choosing to wear overalls, operate one of the processing plants, and go out to catch mussels.

top right Benny getting ready to cast off from the sunny painted harbor of Nykøbing on the island of Mors in the Limfjord.

bottom right The small mussel boats are painted with a bright palate of pale blue, red, white, and green. Many of the hulls of these boats are made from copper. With the bright Nordic sunlight reflecting off the still water of the harbor, it makes for a dazzling scene.

"We use a traditional method of harvesting wild mussels that has been practiced here for generations."

top left Benny works his boat single-handed; he says that "there is not much for an assistant to do" and for that he would have to pay them a quarter of his catch.

bottom left The net full of mussels is dipped in and out of the water like a teabag to clean any excess mud from the shellfish. Mud increases the weight of the catch but a weight that he will not be paid for.

top right Rarely without his pipe, Benny looks as if his boat is only just big enough for him—no wonder he does not want an assistant; there is only room for one.

All of the 28 painted boats that catch mussels for Vilsund are privately owned. The shellfish are processed in local plants and sold to markets all over Europe, Russia, and the Middle East. The fishery works closely with biologists. The mussels are harvested in places where they are plentiful, but if an area is suffering it is left alone until the biologists confirm that the population has recovered. It can be likened to a farmer leaving his field fallow, so that it regains the nutrient levels to support the crops naturally.

Retailers are showing great interest in the mussels, particularly with the possibility that they may soon be MSC-certified. Bart van Olphen of Fishes believes that if the fishery is certified, retailers would be willing to pay a higher premium for the product. He is currently working closely with the WWF to launch a campaign for restaurants to become MSC-certified as well. The aim is to have 5,000 of them on board with the hope that the restaurants will pass on the benefits of certification to the fishermen, but he says it is too early to be sure. The mussels attracted a great deal of attention at the European Seafood Exposition in Brussels in April 2009. Vilsund does not intend to respond to any increase in demand by upping the quantity of mussels they harvest. If there is an increase, they plan to divert more resources to the sale of fresh mussels at the expense of cooked ones.

Benny is the foreman of the mussel fishermen and has been selling shellfish to Vilsund for 29 years. There were already strict controls in place about where in the Limfjord mussels could be gathered at different times of year and how many tons each boat could harvest. Benny is from the fifth generation of a family of fishermen. He worked in the harbor as a young boy and first went out fishing when he was 14. He says, "The methods have changed a little, but essentially I am fishing in the same way as my great-great-grandfather." If he and the other local fishermen had not established such strong self-enforced rules to protect the marine environment, Benny is doubtful that there would still be mussels in the Limfjord. He would be delighted to achieve MSC certification because it would "prove what we have been saying all along—that this

is a sustainable fishery. The most important thing that has changed in the last few years is the awareness of the fishermen. They now realize that they must not impact on nature." The greatest threat to the fishery now is too few young people choosing to go into the industry.

To thank Benny for showing us the Limfjord, Bart and I decided to cook some mussels for him on board his boat. I had heard of a great Danish dish where the mussels are steamed with fresh dill and aquavit (a clear, fiery, schnapps-like spirit distilled from caraway seeds). The boat was the perfect location for the meal and the mussels were spectacular. The acidity of the aquavit cut through the sweet fattiness of the shellfish and wonderfully enhanced their flavor. Served with a good Riesling chilled in the Limfjord, the mussels were devoured by everyone except Benny. He tried a couple and said they were good but opted instead for some aquavit in a glass. As he re-lit his pipe, he explained that he had eaten so many mussels in his life, he was "full to the brim with them." There is no pretense with fishermen and this makes them an exceptionally likeable group of people.

There seems to be no shortage of local interest in the natural harvest of the Limfjord. In return, Vilsund supports and sponsors numerous community events and art projects. Huge mussel sculptures by local artists are dotted around the shoreline in harbors and villages throughout the Limfjord. I counted at least four mussel and shellfish fairs held in and around the fjord during the spring and summer. Løgstør, the island of Fur, and the harbor in Nykøbing all have their own festivals, in which the mighty mussel is celebrated in music and art, and with lots of

above The small plump mussels of the Limfjord fill their shells and are heavy for their size. They are smaller than some of their European cousins but their meat is deliciously firm and sweet.

above Bart and I tuck into our second pan of mussels of the afternoon, these ones washed down with some good local beer. The recipe with the aquavit was a real winner with everyone who tried it.

over-eating and drinking. At the annual Mussel Festival in Løgstør in July 2009, Vilsund Trading received the town's golden key for the support it has given the community over the last five years.

Vilsund is involved in various projects to educate people about the traditional mussel harvesting methods used in the Limfjord. The firm recently welcomed a group of 250 children to its factory to learn about sustainability. Local people want to stay in the area and the company helps them do it. Vilsund offers its employees flexible working hours to suit family life, provides them with breakfast and lunch, and pays about 60 percent more than the minimum wage.

As well as returning smaller mussels alive to the fjord, Vilsund grinds up their empty shells for local farmers to use as fertilizer. Other shells are used for eco-building. As they trap and store heat, they make excellent insulation material. They are also very efficient filterers. If wastewater and unwanted odors are pumped through containers of mussel shells, they emerge cleansed. Vilsund has established a nice little sideline selling shells to companies that require industrial filtration. The possibility of MSC certification for the Vilsund fishery offers the prospect of both recognition and reward for these numerous ways of utilizing mussels.

Aquavit is a clear Danish spirit that is often enjoyed with seafood dishes. It is flavored with caraway seeds and has a similar strong taste to the French pastis or Greek ouzo. Either of these two spirits could be substituted for the aquavit. The fresh dill and caraway seeds cut through the richness of the mussels, and you can add a little extra flavoring if you serve these mussels with some fresh dill mayonnaise.

danish mussels with dill and aquavit

Serves 2 to 4

1 tablespoon oil
2 fresh bay leaves
¼ teaspoon crushed hot red pepper
1 teaspoon caraway seeds
1 onion, finely chopped
bunch of fresh dill, coarsely chopped
4 sprigs of fresh flat-leaf parsley,
    coarsely chopped
⅓ cup dry white wine
salt and freshly ground black pepper
5 tablespoons aquavit
3½lb mussels, cleaned and debearded

For the dill mayonnaise
2 egg yolks
1 teaspoon Dijon mustard
1 teaspoon red wine vinegar
1 cup extra virgin olive oil
juice of ½ lemon
handful of fresh dill, chopped

Heat the oil in a large saucepan over medium to high heat. Add the bay leaves, crushed hot red pepper, and caraway seeds. Cook for 1 minute until fragrant and aromatic. Add the onion, reduce the heat, and cook for 5 minutes without letting it color.

Add half the dill, half the parsley, and all the wine and bring to a boil.

When you are ready to cook the mussels, add a pinch of salt, some pepper, and the aquavit to the broth. Add the cleaned mussels, cover, and cook over medium to high heat until the shells have opened, about 4 to 5 minutes.

Meanwhile, make the dill mayonnaise. Drop the egg yolks into a bowl with the mustard, a little salt, and the vinegar. Stir to combine. Gradually pour in the oil, drop by drop and stirring all the time. Continue stirring until all the oil is used up and you have a thick emulsion. Stir in the lemon juice and the chopped dill. Season to taste with salt and pepper.

Remove the mussels from the heat and discard any shells that remain closed. Garnish the dish with the remaining dill and parsley and serve the mussels in large bowls with the dill mayonnaise and lots of fresh bread, or a bowl of hot fries. Once you have tried them, you will see that mussels and fries are a great combination; they are also a good way of soaking up all the lovely liquid in the bottom of the dish. On the boat in the Limfjord we had these sweet mussels with an ice cold Riesling that we had chilled in the harbor. The characteristic acidity of the chilled wine cuts through the richness of the shellfish.

There are many variations of baked mussels, which are a delicious starter when served with lots of crusty bread. This version comes from southern Italy and has all the robust characteristics of the region. As ever, it is important to use good-quality tomatoes that are really ripe and juicy and lots of fresh herbs.

cozze al gratin (mussels gratin)

Serves 4 to 6

extra virgin olive oil
2 garlic cloves, finely chopped
½ bunch of fresh basil, stems and leaves separated
3 sprigs of fresh oregano or marjoram, stems and leaves separated
3½lb mussels, cleaned and debearded
⅓ cup crisp dry white wine
3 slices of crusty white bread
3 sprigs of fresh flat-leaf parsley
salt and freshly ground black pepper
4 large ripe tomatoes, coarsely chopped
juice of ½ lemon
lemon wedges, to serve

Heat a large heavy-bottomed pan over high heat. Add a little oil, half the garlic, and the basil and oregano or marjoram stems. Add the mussels and the wine. Cover with a lid and cook over high heat, shaking the pan a couple of times so the shellfish cook evenly. Cook until all the mussels have opened, about 4 to 5 minutes. Discard any that are still closed. Remove the pan from the heat and strain the mussels, reserving the juice.

Place the bread and half the leaves of basil and oregano or marjoram with half the parsley in a food processor. Pulse until you have fine herb breadcrumbs. Heat 4 tablespoons of olive oil in a heavy-bottomed pan over medium to high heat. When it is hot, add the breadcrumbs and fry until golden brown, aromatic, and crisp. Season with salt and black pepper and cook for a few minutes more until a light golden brown color. Remove from the pan, strain, and then place on paper towels to absorb the excess oil. (This fried breadcrumb mixture is known as *pangrattato* and is a wonderful addition on top of seafood pasta dishes from southern Italy and Sicily.)

Heat another saucepan over medium heat, add a little oil and the remaining garlic, and cook until golden brown. Coarsely chop the remaining herbs and add to the pan. Cook for another minute, then add the tomatoes and cook over low heat for 10 minutes until they have cooked down.

Preheat the oven to 350°F.

Meanwhile, strain the shellfish cooking liquid into the tomato mixture through a piece of muslin placed inside a fine sieve. Turn up the heat and simmer until the liquid has reduced and the sauce has thickened. Mix in the lemon juice, taste and adjust the seasoning, and then stir in half of the fried breadcrumbs.

Lay the mussels out in a large ovenproof dish and remove the top shells so you are left with the meat in half shells. Spoon the finished tomato mixture into each shell to cover the mussels. Scatter the remaining herb breadcrumbs over the stuffed mussels. Bake for 5 minutes. Serve immediately with lemon wedges and lots of fresh bread to soak up all the juice and clean out the stuffed shells.

The seafood dishes of Catalonia are second to none. They are bold and vibrant and packed full of flavors that taste of the sun and the sea. A sofrito is a tomato and onion sauce that is cooked slowly to make it really sweet. This is a foundation of Catalan cooking. There are as many recipes and variations for sofrito as there are Latin American and Spanish cooks. Latin American sofritos often include cilantro and smoked dried chiles, others use smoked paprika, or saffron, or are very plain. At its most simple, this Spanish classic will consist of tomatoes, olive oil, and sweet onions. It is also used in paellas and other traditional Spanish dishes. In this recipe, the baked mussels are spiked with lots of garlic and ripe tomatoes, with a hint of smoked paprika. They are best served with toasted bread anointed with extra virgin olive oil and rubbed with more garlic. Serve as the first of many small courses on a summer evening with a few bottles of crisp white wine.

baked catalan mussels with tomato, garlic, and olive oil

Serves 4 to 6

For the sofrito
3 large ripe tomatoes
olive oil
3 red onions, grated
1 teaspoon sugar
salt and freshly ground black pepper
½ teaspoon Spanish smoked
   sweet paprika
2 bay leaves
pinch of crushed hot red pepper flakes

3 tablespoons olive oil
3 garlic cloves, finely chopped, plus
   1 whole clove for rubbing
3½lb mussels, cleaned and
   debearded
½ cup crisp dry white wine
1 small bunch of fresh parsley, chopped
crusty white bread
extra virgin olive oil
juice of 1 lemon

First make the sofrito. Cut the tomatoes in half. Place a grater over a large mixing bowl and rub the open face of the tomatoes over the grater until all the flesh is grated. Discard the skin that stays in your palm.

Heat 2 tablespoons of olive oil in a pan over low to medium heat. Add the grated onions, sugar, and a large pinch of salt and cook, stirring occasionally with a wooden spoon, until the onions become soft, tender, and begin to caramelize, about 30 minutes.

Add the grated tomato pulp, paprika, bay leaves, and red pepper flakes. Increase the heat to medium to high and cook for 10 minutes more. The sofrito will be ready when the tomato has broken down and deepened in color, and the oil has separated from the sauce.

Preheat the oven to 400°F. When ready to bake the mussels, heat a large, shallow ovenproof pan or flameproof casserole over medium to high heat. Add the olive oil and the chopped garlic. Spread the mussels out across the pan. Add the white wine, then spoon over the tomato sofrito. Add half of the parsley and season with salt and black pepper.

Transfer the pan to the oven and bake until the mussels have opened, about 5 minutes. (Discard any that do not.) While the mussels are cooking, grill or toast slices of bread, then rub them with a little garlic and dollop with some good-quality extra virgin olive oil.

Remove the mussels from the oven and scatter over the remaining parsley. Squeeze the lemon juice over the top and serve with the toasted bread.

Moules mariniere is probably one of the simplest and most famous ways of serving mussels. This dish is at its best without complicated additions; the delicious sweetness of the mussels and the slightly savory juice that they release are therefore allowed to shine. Use a good crisp white wine to open the shellfish, and cook only with a wine that you would like to drink yourself. For the complete experience, serve this simple classic with lots of chilled Sancerre or Vouvray.

mussels with parsley and white white

Serves 2 to 4

3½lb mussels
2 tablespoons butter
1 onion, finely chopped
1 bouquet garni (bay leaves, thyme, and
    parsley stems tied up with string)
¾ cup crisp dry white wine
salt and freshly ground black pepper
4 sprigs of fresh flat-leaf parsley,
    coarsely chopped

Thoroughly clean the mussels and remove the beards. With an old kitchen knife, remove any bits of barnacles on the shell. Discard any mussels that do not close when tapped, or that are broken or smell. Rinse the mussels under cold running water.

Heat the butter in a large saucepan over medium to high heat. Add the onion and the bouquet garni. Reduce the heat and cook for 5 minutes without letting the onion color.

Add the cleaned mussels and the wine to the saucepan. Season with a little salt and black pepper and add half the parsley. Tightly cover the pan with a lid and cook over medium to high heat until the shells have opened, about 4 to 5 minutes. Give the pan a good shake a couple of times to ensure that the mussels are cooking evenly.

Remove the mussels from the heat and discard any shells that remain closed. Transfer the mussels into a colander, then strain the liquid through a piece of muslin and a fine sieve to remove any grit or sand. Pour the strained juice into a clean pan and taste. Add a little more salt and black pepper, if necessary, and add the remaining parsley. Serve the mussels in large shallow bowls with the juice spooned over the top, accompanied by lots of fresh bread to mop up all the good bits and tasty juice.

These delicious fritters are best eaten hot and fresh from the pan as a great start to a summer evening meal. They have a subtle but complex flavor: the mussels are sweet, the pepper flakes and black pepper are hot and, when served with lemon wedges, they have a sourness that brings everything into balance.

sicilian mussel fritters

Serves 6 to 8

olive oil, for frying
2¼lb mussels, cleaned and debearded
⅓ cup white wine
lemon wedges, to serve

For the batter
1½ cups self-rising flour
2 eggs
⅓ cup milk
1 medium onion, finely chopped
2 garlic cloves, finely chopped
pinch of crushed hot red pepper flakes
salt and freshly ground black pepper
3 sprigs of fresh basil, coarsely chopped
grated zest of 1 lemon

Heat a little oil in a heavy-bottomed pan over medium to high heat. Add the mussels and the wine and cover with a lid. Quickly steam the mussels for about 3 to 5 minutes, then remove the pan from the heat and strain the mussels into a colander. Keep the mussel liquid for another dish, such as a pasta dish, risotto, or fish stew.

Allow the mussels to cool, then remove them from their shells (discard any that do not open). Coarsely chop the mussel meat and set it aside.

To make the batter, sift the self-rising flour into a bowl. Make a well in the center and add the eggs. Gently whisk the milk into the mixture, incorporating all the flour. Keep whisking to get rid of the lumps until you have a thick smooth batter the consistency of heavy cream. Add the onion and the mussel meat to the batter.

In a pestle and mortar, pound the garlic, pepper flakes, and a pinch of salt together to form a paste. Add the basil and continue to pound until smooth. Spoon this green purée into the batter and add the lemon zest; season with salt and black pepper.

Heat enough oil in a high-sided pan to shallow-fry the fritters. When the oil is hot, fry a sample of the fritter mixture by dropping it into the pan and cooking it for 2 minutes until golden brown on both sides. Taste and adjust the seasoning. There is nothing worse than cooking a whole batch having not tasted the mix first.

To cook the fritters, drop 1 tablespoon of the mixture for each one into the hot oil. Cook the fritters in batches of about 8 at a time so that the oil stays hot. Cook until golden brown on one side. Using 2 spoons, flip the fritters over. The total cooking time for each fritter should be about 3 minutes. Continue until you have used all of the mixture. Drain the fritters on paper towels and serve on a large platter with wedges of lemon.

This delicious seafood risotto is rich and creamy, but it also has a little acidity to give it a perfect balance of taste. The thin shavings of fennel that are added right at the end provide fantastic additional texture.

mussel and fennel risotto

Serves 4 to 6

For the fish stock

**white fish bones, cleaned, until the water
is running clear**
1 onion, coarsely chopped
1 leek, white part only, coarsely chopped
2 celery ribs, coarsely chopped
1 garlic bulb
20 black peppercorns
4 bay leaves
3 parsley stems
1 sprig of fresh thyme

For the risotto

2 tablespoons olive oil
**1 onion, finely diced (save half for
the risotto)**
3½lb mussels, cleaned and debearded
⅓ cup white wine
2 garlic cloves
½ teaspoon crushed hot red pepper flakes
2 teaspoons fennel seeds, crushed
**1 bulb fennel, ½ finely diced, ½ cut
into thin slivers (save any fennel
fronds to garnish the risotto)**
2 celery ribs, finely diced
**4 ripe tomatoes, seeded and coarsely
chopped**
1 cup risotto rice
salt and freshly ground black pepper
**½ bunch of fresh flat-leaf parsley,
coarsely chopped**
juice of 1 lemon

First make the stock. Add all the ingredients to a pan, pour in enough cold water to cover, and then bring to a boil. Turn down the heat and simmer for 20 minutes. Skim regularly with a ladle. The fish stock should be sweet and clear, not cloudy and bitter.

Next make the risotto. Heat a large heavy-bottomed pan over high heat. When it is hot add a little of the oil and half the onion. Cook for 1 minute. Add the mussels, the white wine, and 1 ladle of the fish stock. Cover with a lid and cook over high heat, shaking the pan a couple of times so the shellfish cook evenly. Cook for about 4 to 5 minutes until all the mussels have opened. Discard any that are still closed.

Remove the pan from the heat and strain the mussels, reserving the juice. You can use the pan again for the risotto, but rinse it first as there will be grit in the bottom, which would ruin your finished dish.

In a pestle and mortar crush the garlic, pepper flakes, and fennel seeds to make a paste. Heat some oil in the heavy-bottomed pan and cook for 2 minutes until fragrant and aromatic. Add the diced fennel, celery, and remaining onion and lower the heat. Cook gently without coloring for 10 to 12 minutes.

Meanwhile, remove the mussels from the shells and set aside. Throw away three-quarters of the shells, but keep a few in their shells to use as a garnish if you wish. Discard any mussels that did not open. Heat the reserved mussel juice in a small pan.

Add the chopped tomatoes and the rice to the cooked vegetables and stir so each grain of rice is coated with the moisture and oil. Line a fine sieve with a piece of muslin and strain the mussel juice through it. When all the moisture in the pan has been absorbed, add the strained mussel liquid and stir until absorbed. Add the hot stock one ladle at a time. Stir the rice after each addition until the liquid has been absorbed.

Cook the rice until it is *al dente*, about 20 minutes. When ready to serve, add the mussels to the risotto with the thin slivers of raw fennel. (You could also add other seafood such as shrimp or crabmeat.) Add most of the chopped parsley with the lemon juice, and check the seasoning very carefully. Garnish with the remaining parsley and some chopped fennel fronds. Serve the risotto immediately; otherwise the residual heat in the pan will continue to cook the rice and it will become dense and sticky.

south africa hake

Species: hake (*Merluccius paradoxus* and *merluccius capensis*)
Certification: April 2004
Location: South Atlantic Ocean
Fishing methods: bottom trawl
Fishery tonnage: 134,000 metric tons
Vessels: deep-sea trawlers ranging from 65 to 300 feet
   in length and inshore trawlers ranging from 50 to 115 feet

south africa hake

The fishing port of Cape Town is dominated by large trawlers and the huge fish-processing plant of Irvin & Johnson Seafood, which is the biggest in the country. The industrial appearance contrasts strongly with small scale, picturesque ports such as Hastings. But the enormous vessels very near to downtown Cape Town are certainly impressive. Hake fishing here is big business. The ships catch thousands of tons of the fish every day. They are gutted by hundreds of hands, mainly women's, whose husbands are often out at sea catching the fish. Hake is filleted for sending fresh or processed into frozen fish products such as fish fingers and white fish burgers that end up on the shelves of European and American supermarkets. Thanks to MSC certification, the market for fresh hake has grown rapidly over the last few years and beautiful and tasty white fillets and whole hake are now in demand in places such as Spain and the Netherlands.

   The Cape Town fishermen of Irvin & Johnson Seafood are well aware that visitors might believe that industrial fishing and sustainability are incompatible. As a result, they welcome guests to their plants and on board their trawlers, and are happy to demonstrate that it is possible to catch large quantities without undermining fish stocks. In this respect, African fishermen are much further ahead than their European counterparts. Suggestions that they are doing something unusual are met with bafflement, as they understand that without abundant fish stocks, they will be out of a job.

   The Cape Town fishermen know what they are talking about. They have been catching hake from the coastal waters off South Africa and Namibia—where the cold and warm currents of the Atlantic and Indian Oceans converge—for over a hundred years, using large-meshed trawl nets that allow undersize hake and other fish to escape. A trawl is a long tunnel-shaped net with a wide open mouth and a closed tail where the fish is collected while it is dragged along the sea bottom or through the water. At the end of the 1960s, however, the international fishing fleet began to cast its nets here too. The Cape Town hake fishermen were faced with a stark choice: to join in the plunder of the fishing grounds, or to change course completely. They chose the latter, becoming the first hake fishery to be certified as sustainable. They are also the only African fishery to receive MSC certification. In 2008, the MSC opened an African office in Cape Town and together with the WWF they are looking for opportunities to have more fisheries certified not only in South Africa, but also in countries such as Mozambique, Ghana, and Madagascar. From the consumer's perspective, MSC-certified fish is amazingly popular in South

top right One of Irvin & Johnson Seafood's ships moves through the darkness toward the rich fishing grounds on the Atlantic Ocean near Cape Town.

bottom right Two fishermen prepare the huge nets for the next successful catch.

"How else could you fish? If you catch all the fish in the ocean, you're out of a job."

top left Despite the hard work, the fishermen have time to share a joke on deck.

bottom left Workers at the Irvin & Johnson Seafood processing plant. The majority of the staff are women, whose husbands are often out at sea catching the fish.

top right A fresh catch of shiny hake ready to be processed into various MSC-certified products.

Africa. In almost every good restaurant you will find the WWF green/red list of fish species indicating which species are sustainable, and MSC products are widely available through the main retailers. However, there are still problems on the horizon. Spanish fishermen, capitalizing on an insatiable demand for *merluza* in their home country, pay large sums of money to secure hake quotas from people who do not even own ships. A lot of fish is still caught illegally by European and Asian fishermen, and rich countries buy up all the legitimate permits. African governments think they are doing good business, but they probably have little idea how much profit the Europeans are making.

Despite the competition, being a fisherman in Cape Town remains an escape route out of poverty. Crews are away from home a large part of the year, but life on board is pleasant enough. The men are well fed—"Three meals a day, what more do you want?"—and they are able to put aside some money. They are also allowed to take home 45 pounds of fish every month. Some of the men, such as Tom, are planning to stay ashore in the future. He has calculated how many years he will have to fish in order to finance a university education. He and other young men jump for joy each time a full net is hauled in, as more fish means more income. Without the hake, such opportunities would be denied them.

The day we sail out with Captain Ronnie and his crew, the catch is disappointing. On the bridge, Captain Ronnie explains the reason: "We are sailing in green water, which has fewer fish. Hake mainly occurs in blue water. The different colors are caused by two sea currents. Off the South African coast, the cold current from the Antarctic and the currents from the Atlantic and Indian Oceans meet." The converging currents also determine the characteristic climate of Cape Town: in the morning the wind is very strong, but a few hours later there is a clear blue sky and not a breath of wind. The fishermen here catch two species: the deep-water hake and a variety found in shallow waters. Deep-water hake is predominantly targeted by the large-meshed trawl nets that can reach down to where it lurks at the bottom of the ocean, while the shallow-water variety is largely caught by inshore trawl, longline, and handline methods. The ship's bridge

has been equipped with some impressive equipment, such as the "spreaders," which allow the captain to adjust the mouth width of the net. Another speciality piece of equipment measures the quantity of fish inside it. The rules dictate that Captain Ronnie must not exceed six metric tons. A colored chart on a screen tells him whether the fish that have entered the net are mainly large or small.

The crew consists of a total of 15 fishermen and as soon as daylight breaks, the fishing starts in earnest. Huge nets collect the hake from the ocean floor, and on the lower deck the processing of the fish starts by grading the catch into the different boxes. The working day lasts for as long as it is light and the men can be at sea for up to five days in a row. When they return to land the fish in the harbor, they will often leave again the same day. After having done three trips in a row, they are allowed a few days off. Despite the long hours and time away from their families and friends, they are happy with their jobs. In comparison to other jobs in South Africa they are well paid and taken care of by their employer. All are working hard to save some money for the future.

Once we are back on shore we spend some time among the fishermen from the smaller boats. Cape Town and its surroundings is a paradise for fish lovers and enthusiastic fishermen can be found in small ports such as Kalk Bay in Fish Hoek. They also catch hake but are looking further afield for other species such as squid because they like its taste. Some just come back with boats full of crayfish. Anything left over will be used as bait the following day. On the pier

above Harbor life on the pier of Kalk Bay where fishermen try their luck without leaving dry land. The streams drive some fish toward the coast.

above A small part of the catch is saved for the fishermen's own consumption, cooked with just a bit of seasoning. Where better to enjoy a freshly caught meal than in the picturesque harbor of Kalk Bay?

of the harbor, I meet Martin. He is preparing his freshly caught hake on a small wooden board. He tells me he has "six small fishing boats catching all kind of species daily, often surrounded by white sharks." Last week he saw a huge shark here in the harbor looking for some food. He prepares the whole fish in a small pan with some oil and and fresh local herbs. It tastes delicious washed down with a glass of local Sauvignon Blanc from the Stellenbosch region. "Here in South Africa, we really take care of our seas, it is in our hearts. But illegal foreign boats take so many fish that we cannot properly control our resources." When speaking to fishermen like Martin, it is obvious they are passionate about their country's resource; for them the importance of keeping the ecosystem well maintained is self-evident. Many small fishermen like Martin would like to be MSC-certified too, but currently there is no money to pay the fees this would entail.

This is a very refreshing and deliciously spicy soup that is made rustic and hearty with the addition of mini-fishcakes. It is full of clean flavors from the chile, lime leaves, and lemongrass. You can use a combination of fillets of fish in this soup in addition to the fishcakes or shrimp or clams.

spicy ocean broth with lemongrass and herb fishcakes

Serves 4 to 6

2 quarts fish stock
1 tablespoon olive oil
2 garlic cloves, finely chopped
2 lemongrass stems, tough outer leaves discarded, finely chopped
5 slices of fresh ginger
2 medium-hot red chiles, seeded and finely chopped
2 sprigs of cilantro, stems finely chopped
2 medium onions, finely chopped
3 kaffir lime leaves
2 tablespoons tamarind paste, dissolved in 5 tablespoons hot water
juice of 1 orange
2 tablespoons fish sauce
14oz hake fillet, cleaned, skinned, and cut into ¾in cubes
salt and freshly ground black pepper
juice of 2 limes

For the fishcakes
14oz hake fillet, cleaned, skinned, and cut into ¾in cubes
grated zest of 1 lime
3 sprigs of fresh mint
3 sprigs of fresh Thai basil
1 medium-hot red chile, seeded and finely chopped
3 scallions, finely chopped
2 sprigs of cilantro, stems finely chopped, leaves reserved for the garnish
salt and freshly ground black pepper
⅓ cup oil, for frying

First make the fish stock using the cleaned bones of the hake, or bones from another firm white-fleshed fish. The flavors of the soup will be strong, so the fish stock does not have to be Asian. If you don't have any fish stock, use chicken or vegetable stock.

Next make the fishcakes. Place the fish in a food processor and add all the other ingredients except the oil, reserving half the scallions and the cilantro leaves to garnish the finished soup. Season the mixture well with salt and black pepper. Purée the ingredients for the cakes to a coarse paste.

Take a small piece of the mixture and fry until golden brown. Taste and adjust the seasoning if necessary, then lightly oil your hand and roll the fish mixture into small balls, no bigger than a ping pong ball. Set aside.

Bring the stock to a boil in a saucepan. Heat 1 tablespoon of oil in another large pan over medium to high heat. Add the garlic, lemongrass, and ginger. Cook quickly until they are fragrant and aromatic to caramelize the flavors, about 3 minutes. Add the chiles and the cilantro stems. Cook for another minute, then add the onions, reduce the heat, and cook until softened, about 5 minutes. Add the hot stock and the lime leaves. Gently simmer for about 10 minutes. Add the tamarind liquid, the orange juice, and the fish sauce.

While the soup is simmering, lightly fry the fishcakes. Heat a little oil in a frying pan over medium to high heat. Cook the fishcakes in small batches until golden brown. Flatten the fishcakes slightly with a spatula while cooking. You are not cooking them all the way through, just sealing them on the outside. The fishcakes will continue cooking in the fish soup.

Season the diced fish with salt and black pepper and add to the soup with the lightly fried fishcakes. Gently simmer for 3 minutes—be careful that they do not break up. Turn off the heat and allow the fish and fishcakes to cook through in the residual heat of the soup. Make sure that you do not overcook the fish or it will be tough.

Add the lime juice and serve garnished with the reserved cilantro leaves and chopped scallions.

Grilled white fish is given added flavor with a fantastic South Indian masala marinade. The marinating paste is bold and robust, containing green chile and lots of cilantro as well as dried spices such as coriander seeds, cloves, black pepper, and turmeric. The fresh green mango salsa served with it provides a punchy, vibrant contrast of flavors, textures, and colors. All the elements of hot, sweet, salty, and sour are present, and the many shades of green contrast with the whiteness of the fish.

indian masala-grilled fish
with green mango salsa

Serves 4

4 fillets of hake or other sustainable firm white-fleshed fish, weighing about 7oz each
seeds from 4 green cardamom pods
4 cloves
1 teaspoon ground turmeric
1 teaspoon black peppercorns
1 tablespoon coriander seeds
6 green chiles, seeded and finely chopped
5 garlic cloves, finely chopped
1½in piece of ginger, peeled and finely chopped
small bunch of cilantro leaves, stems finely chopped (reserve half the leaves for the mango salsa)
1 onion, finely chopped
¼ cup water
juice of ½ lemon
salt and freshly ground black pepper
2 tablespoons vegetable oil

Score the fish fillets with four diagonal slits about ½in deep on the rounded presentation side.

Place a frying pan over medium heat and dry-fry the spices until fragrant and aromatic, about 2 minutes. In a pestle and mortar, or in a spice grinder, crush the toasted spices.

Mix together the green chiles, garlic, ginger, and cilantro stems and place the mixture in a blender or food processor. Process the mixture to a paste. Add the onion, the toasted spices, and the water. Purée until completely smooth. Add half the cilantro leaves (save the other half for the mango salsa) and the lemon juice and combine. Taste and season well with salt and pepper. Spread the marinade over the fish and leave to marinate for 30 to 40 minutes.

While the fish is marinating, start the salsa (see recipe, opposite). In a bowl, mix the shallots with the mangoes and chiles and sprinkle with the salt. Set aside for 30 minutes.

Preheat a griddle pan over medium heat. Make the foil envelopes: tear off four lengths of tin foil, about 3 feet each. Fold each piece in half so that you have a double layer that is 1½ feet long. Fold the pieces in half again and open them back up, so they look like an open book. Splash a little vegetable oil on the right side of each foil "book." Place the pieces of fish on top of the oil with a little extra paste and season with salt and black pepper. Fold the other side of the "book" over the top of the fish, then fold over the long-sided edge twice— you want a tightly sealed parcel with an open short side. These fish parcels can be prepared up to an hour before cooking.

Preheat the oven to 400°F. Seal the final side of each envelope and place them on the griddle pan for 2 minutes, then transfer to the oven for another 8 to 10 minutes, depending on the thickness of the fish. (If cooking a small to medium whole fish, bake in the oven for 20 minutes.)

For the green mango salsa
5 shallots, halved, core removed, and finely sliced
2 unripe mangoes, peeled and cut into ½in dice
2 green chiles, seeded and finely chopped
2 teaspoons sea salt
½ teaspoon fenugreek seeds
1 teaspoon coriander seeds
2 tablespoons vegetable oil
1 tablespoon mustard seeds
pinch of crushed hot red pepper flakes
½ teaspoon ground turmeric
juice of 2 limes

While the fish is cooking, finish the salsa. Heat a small pan over medium heat and dry-fry the fenugreek and coriander seeds until fragrant and aromatic, about 2 to 3 minutes. Grind the toasted seeds in a pestle and mortar. Heat the oil in a heavy-bottomed saucepan over medium to high heat. Add the mustard seeds and stir until they start to pop, about 30 seconds. Add the hot red pepper flakes and turmeric and any liquid from the salted mangoes. Heat vigorously for 2 minutes until the spices are fragrant and aromatic. Chop the reserved cilantro leaves.

Pour the spice mixture over the mangoes. Stir together with the lime juice and most of the chopped cilantro leaves, and adjust the salt to taste. You should have a refreshing balance of hot, sweet, salty, and sour, but if it is not sour enough, add a little more lime juice. Allow the mixture to cool, then taste again and season if necessary.

When ready to serve, transfer the parcels to plates and allow your guests to open them so they get all the aromas. (Be careful with the steam, because it may come out in a jet.) Garnish with the remaining chopped cilantro leaves and serve with the green mango salsa.

Hake is a magnificent yet underrated fish, except in Spanish and French kitchens where it is featured more often, and rightly so. Hake flakes into a soft texture but has a meaty flavor. It works very well cooked on the bone, either in steaks or whole. The natural gelatin that is in the bones keeps the fish moist when cooking and the bones hold in the shape and all the flavor of the fish. Here roasted steaks are served with roasted sliced beets and a coarse salsa verde. This colorful dish just oozes summer.

roasted hake with golden beets and salsa verde

Serves 4 to 6

8 medium-sized beets (a selection of golden, red, and tiger-striped if possible)
olive oil
salt and freshly ground black pepper
2 garlic cloves
sprig of fresh thyme
½ cup water
10½oz beets, Swiss chard, rainbow chard, or baby spinach leaves, rinsed
juice of ½ lemon
whole hake, weighing about 4½lb to 5½lb, scaled, cleaned and cut into 1in thick slices through the bone (ask your fishmonger to do this for you)

For the salsa verde
1 garlic clove
2 tablespoons capers, rinsed
4 sprigs of fresh basil
3 sprigs of fresh mint
4 sprigs of fresh flat-leaf parsley
juice of ½ lemon
2 tablespoons red wine vinegar
4 tablespoons extra virgin olive oil

Preheat the oven to 400°F. Wash and scrub the beets and place in a roasting pan with a little oil, salt, and black pepper. Coarsely chop the garlic and the thyme and add to the roasting pan with the water. (This will keep the beets moist when cooking.) Seal the pan with tin foil, making sure there are no gaps. Roast for 45 minutes or until soft when pierced with a sharp knife. Leave the oven on for roasting the fish.

To make the salsa verde, place the garlic and capers in a food processor or a pestle and mortar and blend until smooth. Add all the herbs, then coarsely purée until you have a coarse green paste. Add the lemon juice and vinegar, transfer the mixture to a bowl, and stir in the olive oil. Season to taste with salt and black pepper and add more lemon juice if necessary.

Wash and trim the beets, chard, or spinach leaves and blanch for 2 minutes in salted boiling water. You want the stems of the leaves to have bite and not be too mushy. Refresh the leaves under cold running water to stop the cooking and to keep the color fresh. Squeeze out any excess water. When the beets are cooked, cool until just warm. Peel if you wish, but if they are cleaned well before cooking, the skin is edible and delicious. Cut the beets into thin round slices. In a large bowl, combine the warm beet slices and the beet leaves. Add the lemon juice, a splash of olive oil, and season with salt and black pepper.

Heat a large heavy-bottomed sauté pan over medium to high heat. If you are roasting more than four pieces of hake, have a baking sheet ready. Pat the fish dry with paper towels and season. Pour a little olive oil into the pan and add the fish steaks, presentation-side down. Do this in batches to avoid overloading the pan. Cook for 2 to 3 minutes. Do not move the fish around while it is cooking, but gently lift a piece to see if it is crisp and brown. Transfer the steaks to the prepared baking sheet, golden-side up, then slide the fish to the still-hot oven and bake for 7 to 8 minutes.

To serve, arrange the beets and leaves in the center of each plate and place a piece of roasted fish on top. Spoon some salsa verde on to the fish.

This dish is spectacular; rustic, and full of flavor. The fish is poached in a spicy tomato broth with crushed hot red pepper flakes, onion, and bay leaves. The steamed couscous is moistened with the rich tomato broth and the mixed fish and shrimp. Here we've used hake, but any combination of sustainable white fish can be used either whole or in chunks.

sicilian couscous with hake, spiced tomato broth, shrimp, and bay leaves

Serves 6

For the couscous
4 tablespoons olive oil
1 garlic clove, finely chopped
3 fresh bay leaves
1 onion, finely chopped
3 cups couscous
salt and freshly ground black pepper
pinch of crushed hot red pepper flakes
1¾ cups boiling water
3 sprigs of fresh flat-leaf parsley, stems reserved for the fish stock

For the fish stock
2¼lb white fish bones, washed until the water runs clear
1 quart water
2 fresh bay leaves
8 peppercorns
1 onion, coarsely chopped

For the tomato broth
3 tablespoons olive oil
2 onions, finely chopped
1 garlic clove, finely chopped
pinch of crushed hot red pepper flakes
1¾ cups tomato sauce
⅓ cup crisp white wine
large pinch of saffron
2¼lb hake fillet, skinned and cut into ¾in cubes
18oz MSC-certified raw shrimp, peeled and deveined

First make the couscous. Heat half the olive oil in a heavy-bottomed saucepan. Add the garlic and bay leaves and cook for 1 minute until aromatic. Add the onion, reduce the heat, and cook for 5 minutes until softened but not colored. Remove the pan from the heat and add the couscous and the remaining olive oil. Season with salt and black pepper and the red pepper flakes.

Stir so that the couscous grains are seasoned and coated with the oil and onion juices. Add the water and cover with a lid. Let sit for about 10 minutes so that all the liquid and steam are absorbed. Remove the lid and stir with a fork to break up any clumps. Coarsely chop the parsley leaves and mix into the couscous.

To make the fish stock, place the cleaned bones in a deep saucepan. Add all the other ingredients, place over medium heat, and bring to a boil. Skim the stock regularly to remove the foam that rises to the surface. Simmer gently for 20 minutes, then strain through a sieve.

To make the broth, heat the olive oil in a heavy-bottomed saucepan over medium to high heat and add the onions. Cook without coloring for about 5 minutes. Crush the garlic and the pepper flakes in a pestle and mortar with a pinch of salt. Add the garlic paste to the onions and cook for 1 minute. Add the tomato sauce, wine, and saffron and bring to a boil. Season with salt and black pepper. Lower the heat and simmer for 10 minutes to reduce the sauce. Add the fish stock and simmer for another 10 minutes. Check the seasoning.

When ready to cook, season the fish and the shrimp with salt and black pepper and add to the broth. Reduce the heat so that the fish and shrimp are gently poaching and cook for 5 minutes. Remove the fish and shrimp, then turn up the heat to reduce the broth. Taste the broth and adjust the seasoning as needed with salt and black pepper and a little lemon juice, if you wish.

Arrange the couscous on a large warmed platter and spoon the fish and shrimp around the outside. Moisten the couscous with some of the reduced tomato broth. Serve with lots of crusty bread and chilled Italian white wine such as a Soave or Pinot Grigio.

Salsa romesco is a brilliant sauce that covers all the bases for flavors and textures. It contains roasted almonds and hazelnuts, garlic, and smoked paprika. Grilled red peppers and chile are blended with olive oil to make a fabulous paste. It can be served as part of a tapas menu with grilled scallions, or as a dip with crusty bread. Here the portion-sized pieces of hake are marinated in the red nutty salsa before they are roasted in the oven in an authentic terracotta dish. Squeeze a little fresh lemon juice over the top at the end to awaken all the flavors and temper the richness of the sauce and roasted fish.

baked hake with spanish salsa romesco of grilled red peppers, hazelnuts, and paprika

Serves 4

1 dried chile
1 red bell pepper, halved and seeded
⅓ cup olive oil
2 plum tomatoes
1 teaspoon brown sugar
3 garlic cloves
1 thick slice of bread, crusts removed
¼ cup hazelnuts, shelled
¼ cup almonds, blanched
½ fresh red chile, seeded
½ teaspoon sweet smoked paprika
1 tablespoon sherry vinegar, plus extra
    to taste
salt and freshly ground black pepper
juice of ½ lemon
4 hake fillets, weighing about
    8 to 9oz each

Preheat the grill. Cover the dried chile with hot water and leave to soak for 10 minutes or until soft. Brush the red pepper with oil and place on a baking sheet. Cut the tomatoes in half, sprinkle with the sugar, and place on the sheet with the peppers. Grill until the tomatoes are caramelized and the skin of the pepper is blistered and blackened.

Heat 2 tablespoons of the olive oil in a heavy-bottomed pan. Add the whole garlic cloves and sauté until golden. Remove and reserve. Tear the bread into pieces and cook in the garlic-infused oil until golden and crisp.

Dry-fry the hazelnuts and almonds in another pan, until they turn pale golden in color. When the pepper is cool, peel off the skin. Cut the softened chile in half (reserving the soaking liquid), discard the seeds, and finely chop the flesh.

Place the chile in a food processor with the reserved garlic and blend until smooth. Add 2 teaspoons of the soaking liquid. Add the pepper and tomatoes. Add the toasted bread and half of the toasted nuts and purée until smooth. Add the fresh chile, paprika, and the sherry vinegar. Coarsely chop the remaining nuts.

Slowly add the remaining olive oil in a stream and work until it makes a coarse-textured, dip-like paste. Taste and adjust the seasoning if necessary. Add a little lemon juice or sherry vinegar to taste. The sauce should have a smoky heat from the paprika and the dried chile. Stir the remaining nuts into the paste. Pat the fish pieces dry using paper towels and let them marinate in the salsa romesco for 30 minutes.

Meanwhile, preheat the oven to 350°F. Place the pieces of hake skin-side up in a shallow ovenproof terracotta dish. Spoon the rest of the sauce around the fish, with a little on top. Bake for 10 to 12 minutes, depending on the thickness of the fillets.

Remove from the oven, squeeze lemon juice over top, and serve immediately.

This is a simple and delicious way of cooking fish—it produces a heady aromatic steam while cooking, which is released as you open the parcels. If you serve the puffed parcels at the table, your guests can experience the fresh perfume for themselves. This dish is particularly good served with grilled asparagus or braised spinach.

parcel-baked hake with roast tomatoes, scallions, white wine, and parsley

Serves 6

24 cherry tomatoes
extra virgin olive oil
salt and freshly ground black pepper
1 whole hake, weighing about 3lb,
    scaled, cleaned, and gutted
1 bunch of fresh flat-leaf parsley
1 bunch of scallions, finely sliced
¾ cup dry white wine

Preheat the oven to 400°F. Spread the tomatoes on a baking sheet, mix with a splash of olive oil, and season with salt and black pepper. Roast in the oven for 20 minutes.

Meanwhile, cut the hake into 1in thick steaks through the bone—you can ask your fishmonger to do this for you. Chop about one-third of the parsley and set it aside for later.

Tear off six lengths of tin foil, about 3 feet each. Fold each piece in half so that you have a double layer that is 1½ feet long. Fold the pieces in half again and open them back up, so they look like an open book. Lay the six pieces out on a work surface.

Splash a little oil on the right side of each foil "book." Place the pieces of fish on top of the oil and season with salt and black pepper. Scatter the scallions and the leaves of the remaining parsley on and around each piece of fish, add 4 tomatoes per portion, and drizzle with a little oil. Fold the other side of the "book" over the top of the fish, then fold over the long-sided edge a couple of times—you want a tightly sealed parcel with an open short side. These fish parcels can be prepared an hour before cooking.

When you are ready to cook, place some baking sheets in the oven to heat up. Splash some white wine into each fish parcel and seal the final edge. Place the sealed parcels on the preheated baking sheets and bake for 12 minutes. When the fish is cooked, the parcels will be puffed up. With a pair of scissors, cut open two sides of each parcel. Be careful, as the steam inside can come out in a bit of a jet. With a spatula, transfer the fish to serving plates. Spoon the juice and contents of the bag over the fish and garnish with the reserved chopped parsley.

england
dover sole & mackerel

Species: Dover sole and mackerel (*Solea solea* and *Scomber scombrus*)
Certification: September 2005
Location: within the eastern English Channel, between Beachy Head
   and Dungeness and offshore to the 6 mile limit
Fishing methods: trammel net and drift net
Fishery tonnage: 72 metric tons (Dover sole); 10 metric tons (mackerel)
Vessels: under 30 feet, stade-launched from the beach

england dover sole & mackerel

There has been a thriving fishing fleet off the south coast of England since before the Battle of Hastings in 1066. The small wooden boats launched from the beach at Hastings have been operated in much the same way for centuries. They remain virtually unchanged, as do the methods operated by the fishermen. The current modest fleet of 25 or so boats are all less than 30 feet long and are launched at high tide from the stade, which is an Anglo-Saxon word for landing place. As a result, the fleet can go out only in calm conditions, ideally in a prevailing south-westerly breeze. If the wind picks up to force 5 or above, the boats are unable get offshore. This can restrict the number of fishing days for Dover sole to as few as 100 per year, which gives the species a chance to prosper and makes this fishery one of the most environmentally friendly in the country. The Sea Fishing Industry Authority has described the Hastings stade as "as near perfect a fishery as could be devised."

In February, Dover sole start to migrate into the sea around Hastings from deeper waters in the north where they have spent the cold winter months. The season generally starts in March and continues while the fish are spawning, but its length is dependant on the water temperature. Dover sole like to swim in relatively shallow water, with a covering of sand or mud on the bottom in which they can lurk half-buried, watching for passing prey. A breeding stock of Dover sole is endemic to the area of Hastings and Rye. Other significant populations in the English Channel include the Bourgogne and Isle of Wight stocks. "The stock population is going up every year and it is now bigger than in 1957. We wait for the fish to come to us. We cannot go to them as we are small-range and governed by the weather."

To catch sole without trawling the ocean beds, the Hastings fishermen use three-walled static-trammel nets. These have a larger mesh on the outside than on the inside, which ensures that the by-catch is kept to a minimum. The large mesh size is increased throughout the season to ensure that no juveniles are caught, as they are the breeding stock of the future. The sole start to breed when they reach a length of 10in. During the month of April, the fish are heavy with roe. Catching them at this time might seem incompatible with the goal of sustainability, but in fact, the net size ensures that only larger sole that have spawned for a couple of years are targeted, so selling them "roed" does not deplete the breeding stock. By June there are consistent daily catches that continue throughout the summer and autumn. The number of fish usually begins to drop off toward the end of November, but if the water temperature remains high—above 55°F—the sole may stay in the shallower water right up to Christmas.

top right A hot cup of tea is always welcome on board; however, fisherman's brew is an acquired taste. The tea is strong and sweet, and with a slight hint of diesel. Before you taste it, check the rim for dried fish scales, as the two seem to go hand in hand.

bottom right A stade is an Anglo-Saxon name for a landing place, and the wooden boats are landed on the pebbly beach in much the same way as they would have been in 1000 AD.

"It's a case of do or die. I mean, if we don't have enough fish to sustain us, then the whole fishing community around the country will wither and die."

top left A trusty fisherman's knife is never far from reach to prep the landed fish. This is much to the appreciation of the accompanying gaggle of gulls.

bottom left Fishing news is passed from boat to boat by Hastings fishermen in the same way as their ancestors would have done.

top right Graham (l) and Paul (r) share a laugh while relaxing on dry land with a cup of tea.

Paul Joy, who heads up the Hastings fishermen, comes from a traditional fishing family and has been fishing for nearly 40 years. "Our family has been fishing here since 1000 and was here throughout the Spanish Armada. Hastings has been an environmentally friendly fishery for generations and we are still here. We didn't have to adapt for the MSC," says Paul. "We were already there before certification. A lot of people think fishermen are in just it for the short term to make money, but we want to see a future. If any of our children want to carry on with the fishing industry, they've got to have stocks as abundant as when we fished on them." If the Hastings fishermen used larger nets they could catch twenty times more fish, but, as Paul explains, they'd rather allow the sole to grow big enough to breed. Paul regularly stays out at sea for up to 24 hours, anchoring his nets at each end and indicating their locations with marker buoys. Like the rest of the Hastings fishermen, Paul logs everything he catches. He is pleased to be able to say that "we have very few discards."

Unfortunately, only a small percentage of the catch is sold to the MSC-certified Hastings Fish Market Enterprises. The fish concerned are snapped up by some of the top restaurants in London. Bart van Olphen's company Fishes also purchases a significant quantity of the certified Dover sole, but sadly a large proportion of the catch is still sold on the open market without the MSC stamp. These fish sell for a fraction of the price, and as a result the Hastings fishermen are yet to see the full financial benefits of sailing the MSC flag. As Paul says, they need to receive a premium on the price, "so we can say to our fishermen, 'This is the reward for fishing in a sustainable manner.'" To obtain MSC certification, it is necessary to establish a chain of custody that allows the provenance of each fish to be traced back to the boat that caught it. This costs money and it is important that the extra cost is reflected in the price. "We need to be fair to the communities that have historically caught fish and have never endangered the environment.

We need to be fair to the fisherman that fish in a sustainable manner." Inshore coastal fishing communities like this need to be supported. For every fisherman at sea there are 10 jobs on shore. Individual fishmongers, the Hastings fish market, and the 25 hawker vans that sell local fish all over the country are all dependant on the stade. Hopefully, with MSC certification and increased education about the importance of sustainability, small fishing ports like Hastings will be able to survive.

Graham Coglan, port representative and skipper of the *Saint Richard*, has been working the waves for 40 years. He believes that, in the future, the MSC certificate will give him and his colleagues a better return. Fisherman Dean Adams, however, has told his two sons to find another trade. "It's in their blood, but the career path for young fishermen is very hard," he explains. Paul Joy agrees. "It's too unreliable as an income for a family," he says sadly. As public interest in sustainability grows along with demand for products that support the ocean environment, Graham will hopefully be proved right. The paramount need is to educate the customer. When faced with a disparity in the price between sustainable and non-sustainable fish, shoppers will inevitably want to know why they should pay more.

There is another grave problem that faces Paul and his team, as well as many other small inshore coastal fisheries around the country. As their boats are less than 30 feet long, they are not given quotas to fish for cod. Instead, the quotas are awarded to multi-billion dollar

above An MSC-labeled Dover sole that has been caught like this has a chain of custody linked to it, so when sold to the consumer, the fish can be traced back to the boat that caught it.

organizations with larger boats, effectively creating a cartel. Paul is adamant that Channel stocks are very healthy and sustainable as far as small boats are concerned. He reckons that "the cod stocks in the channel are in a better state than at any point in the last 38 years." But because the Hastings boats are not allowed cod quotas, any of the fish that they catch cannot be landed and are thrown back into the sea dead. For the fishermen of Hastings this is heartbreaking, futile, and goes against everything that they stand for. The regulations have also seriously damaged their earnings. Whereas Dover sole is most prolific in the spring and summer months, cod is mostly available in the winter. It used to provide the fishermen with at least 50 percent of their annual income. Many of them are now facing bankruptcy because they are not able to earn a living from a plentiful and sustainable natural resource. There used to be 45 boats fishing from the stade, now the number is 23 and falling. "The small inshore fishing boats make up 93 percent of the country's vessels, have 87 percent of the workforce and 0 percent of the cod quota," states Paul. "Cod fishing in the Channel can be sustainable as long as it is dealt with in the right way," he affirms. In the meantime, the fishermen of the stade face an uncertain future. Despite receiving MSC certification for its Dover sole, mackerel, and herring, this environmentally-friendly fishery has deep concerns for its survival.

In this mouth-watering dish, the Dover sole is flavored with the delicate anise of fennel as thin wedges are added to the fish while cooking. The additional Mediterranean flavors are incorporated as the pan is deglazed with a little white wine, lots of basil, and some lemon juice to create a vibrant and summery sauce. The combination of rich fennel and basil works beautifully with roasted fish, giving it a light and fresh taste.

dover sole with roast fennel

Serves 4 to 6

2 fennel bulbs, trimmed
4 tablespoons olive oil
sea salt and freshly ground
    black pepper
4 to 6 Dover sole, weighing about
    12 to 16oz each, cleaned
⅓ cup crisp white wine
grated zest and juice of 1 lemon
1 tablespoon butter, chopped
½ bunch of fresh basil, coarsely chopped

Cut the fennel bulbs through the heart and finely slice into thin wedges. Heat a saucepan and add 1 tablespoon of the oil. Add the fennel and cook over medium heat until gently browned. Season the fennel with sea salt and black pepper.

Preheat a large frying pan or skillet. Preheat the oven to 400°F and use a little of the oil to grease a roasting pan for the fish. Pat the fish completely dry with paper towels. Rub a little oil on both sides of the fish. Season the fish well with salt and black pepper.

Add a little oil to the hot pan and lay the fish presentation-side down (you will need to do this in batches). It is vital not to move the fish in the pan; if moved, it will not form a golden brown crust. Cook the fish for 4 minutes. Using a spatula, loosen the edges of the fish from the pan and slide the spatula underneath to lift it. Transfer the fish to the prepared roasting pan. If any strips of skin have stuck to the pan, pick them off and put them on the fish.

Wipe out the frying pan with paper towels, return it to the heat, and continue to brown the remaining Dover sole. Once the fish are cooked on the presentation side, arrange the browned fennel around them on the roasting pan and bake in the oven for 5 minutes.

While the fish is baking, deglaze the frying pan with the white wine. Simmer to reduce the wine by one-third and, using a wooden spoon, scrape any bits from the bottom of the pan. Add the lemon zest and, while stirring, drop in the butter piece by piece until the sauce emulsifies. When the fish is cooked, remove from the roasting pan and transfer to a warmed serving platter. Scoop the roasted fennel into the sauce in the pan. Add the chopped basil and the lemon juice and mix to combine. Serve the roasted fish with the sauce spooned over the top, accompanied by a bottle of Pinot Grigio or Soave.

The secret of this dish is to preheat the grill or griddle pan so that it is very hot. The warm dressing contains all the balanced elements of taste: the roasted red peppers are sweet, as is the grilled flesh of the fish; the olives are salty; the hint of crushed chile and the seasoning on the fish is hot and peppery and the lemon juice is sour, which cuts through the richness of the fish. Together they form a stunning picture for the eye and a taste sensation for the palate.

grilled dover sole with a warm dressing of red peppers, thyme, and black olives

Serves 4 to 6

3 red bell peppers
1 tablespoon olive oil, plus extra for oiling the fish
2 garlic cloves, finely chopped
1 small dried chile, crushed
1 tablespoon fresh thyme leaves, chopped
30 pitted black olives, coarsely chopped
¼ cup extra virgin olive oil
juice of 1 lemon
1 tablespoon red wine vinegar
sea salt and freshly ground black pepper
4 to 6 Dover sole, weighing about 12 to 16oz each, cleaned

Grill the peppers until the skin is blackened and blistered, approximately 12 to 15 minutes. Remove from the heat, place in a bowl, cover with plastic wrap, and set aside until cool enough to handle.

Meanwhile, prepare the dressing. Heat the olive oil in a saucepan over medium heat, add the garlic, and cook gently for 2 minutes until the garlic is fragrant, then turn down the heat. Add the chile, thyme, and olives and stir together. Remove from the heat, add the extra virgin olive oil, and set aside.

Peel the skin off the cooled peppers and remove the seeds. If any of the skin or seeds sticks to the flesh, just rinse with a little water. Cut the peppers into thin strips and then into ½in dice. Add to the olive mixture, along with the lemon juice and vinegar. Season the dressing well with salt to taste and lots of black pepper (the olives are salty, so be careful not to over-season). Taste the dressing—it should be sweet, salty, sour, and hot.

Preheat the grill or a griddle pan so that it is extremely hot. Make sure the bars are really clean and, if necessary, re-clean them after cooking each fish. Preheat the oven to 400°F and oil a roasting pan.

Pat the fish completely dry with paper towels. Rub some oil all over, then season well with salt and black pepper. Always cook fish presentation-side down first—in this case, the brown side. Grill for 4 minutes (you will need to do this in batches), then gently transfer the fish to the oiled roasting pan. Do not move or poke the sole, or shake the pan while it is grilling. When you have grilled all the fish on one side, place in the roasting pan presentation side down and cook in the oven for another 5 minutes.

Serve the whole fish with the pepper dressing spooned over the top, and with braised spinach, potatoes, and a salad of mixed greens or arugula.

Roasting a fresh, portion-sized Dover sole on the bone is the best way to capture the impressive flavor of this fish. In this recipe, there is a perfect balance of taste that comes from just a few ingredients. The flesh of the fish is sweet; the chile is hot, and the capers provide saltiness. The accompanying fresh dressing is vibrant and delicious against the simple roasted fish.

roast dover sole with mint, chile, and capers

Serves 4 to 6

4 to 6 Dover sole, weighing about
   12 to 16oz each, cleaned
1 tablespoon olive oil
sea salt and freshly ground
   black pepper
2 garlic cloves, finely chopped
4 tablespoons capers, rinsed
1 lemon, cut into thin slices

For the dressing
1 medium-hot red chile, seeded and
   finely chopped
½ bunch of fresh mint, finely chopped
juice of 1 lemon
¼ cup extra virgin olive oil

Preheat the oven to 400°F and oil a roasting pan for the fish. Preheat a large frying pan or skillet. Pat the fish completely dry with paper towels (this is a very important step before pan-frying and roasting a whole fish), then rub some oil on to the top and bottom of the fish. Season the fish well with sea salt and freshly ground black pepper.

Add a little oil to the hot pan, then lay the fish in the pan presentation-side down (or brown-side up). It is vital not to move the fish in the pan. If moved, it will not form a golden-brown crust. Cook the fish for 4 minutes (you will need to do this in batches). While it is cooking, add the garlic and the capers.

Using a spatula, loosen the edges of the fish from the pan then slide the spatula under the fish carefully to lift it. Transfer the fish to the prepared roasting pan, placing it presentation-side up. If any strips of skin have stuck to the pan, pick them off and put them back on the fish. Arrange a couple of slices of lemon on each sole in the roasting pan and add the capers and garlic. Wipe out the frying pan with paper towels and return it to the heat to cook the other Dover soles. When all the fish is pan-fried, bake the fish in the oven for another 5 minutes.

While the fish is baking, prepare the dressing. In a bowl, mix the chile and mint with the lemon juice and the extra virgin olive oil. Season the dressing with salt and freshly ground black pepper.

When the fish is cooked, remove from the roasting pan. Add the roasted capers and garlic to the dressing and mix. Serve one sole per person on individual plates and spoon the dressing over the fish. Accompany the sole with some simply cooked vegetables or a peppery leaf salad and a cool crisp Riesling. The perfumed taste of the Riesling will complement the combination of chile, mint, and lemon in the dressing.

When I asked the fishermen on the stade in Hastings about how they would like to eat some of their catch, the common thread was "cooked simply." With a fresh Dover sole there is no better way to eat it. In this recipe the whole fish is grilled and served with herb butter, a lemon wedge, and simply grilled leeks. This works perfectly as a spring or early summer dish when the Dover sole are getting really plump. There are no exotic ingredients or elaborate techniques, just good honest food prepared with the minimum of fuss. Perfection.

grilled dover sole with herb butter and grilled leeks

Serves 4 to 6

For the herb butter
½ cup white wine
2 shallots, finely chopped
1 garlic clove, finely chopped
2 sprigs of fresh thyme, finely chopped
2¼ sticks unsalted butter, at room temperature, diced
1 tablespoon red wine vinegar
4 sprigs of fresh parsley, chopped
salt and freshly ground black pepper

4 to 6 whole Dover sole, weighing about 14 to 16oz each, cleaned
4 tablespoons olive oil
salt and freshly ground black pepper
6 medium-sized leeks
1 tablespoon red wine vinegar
lemon wedges, to serve

First make the herb butter. Pour the white wine into a pan and simmer over medium heat with the shallots until the wine has reduced to about 6 tablespoons. Remove from the heat and add the garlic and thyme. When the wine has cooled slightly, add to the butter with the vinegar, parsley, and salt and black pepper. With a fork, mash the butter to incorporate the other ingredients. Taste and add extra salt, black pepper, or garlic if required. Spoon the butter into a bowl.

Pat the fish dry with paper towels and, with a large sharp knife, remove the heads. With a pair of kitchen scissors, remove the fins of the fish. Oil a large grill pan and lay out the fish, brown-side up. Lightly oil the fish and season well with salt and black pepper. Set aside while you cook the leeks.

Trim off the roots of the leeks, leaving a bit of the core to hold them together. Remove the tough outside leaves. Split the leeks in half lengthwise and wash thoroughly. Bring a pan of salted water to a boil and blanch the leeks for about 4 minutes, then refresh in cold water to stop them from cooking and to hold their color. Drain well and place them in a bowl with 1 tablespoon of the olive oil. Season well with salt and pepper. Grill the leeks for 3 minutes until well marked and charred. Return the grilled leeks to the bowl and add another 1 tablespoon of the olive oil, the thyme, and vinegar. Leave to marinate while you cook the fish.

Grill the fish over medium heat for 4 minutes. With a spatula, loosen the edges of the fish from the pan and then carefully slide the spatula under to lift it. Turn the fish over and grill for another 4 minutes on the underside.

When the fish is cooked, transfer each fish to a plate and serve brown-side up with a small pile of the grilled marinated leeks and a lemon wedge. Spoon some of the herb butter over the fish and allow it to melt on the crispy skin.

Fresh oily fish such as mackerel are excellent smoked, and smoked mackerel pâté is famous for this reason. In Thailand, Vietnam, and Singapore, many ingredients are smoked over a mixture of jasmine tea and spices; in this dish the mackerel is smoked using the Asian method to impart a fragrant, spiced aroma. It is served alongside a hot and sour green papaya salad that creates a tastebud explosion on your tongue that's like a firework display going off. Whenever I arrive in Asia, this sort of salad is the first type of dish that I eat—it is spectacular, awakening all the tastebuds and making you aware of where you have landed.

tea-and-cinammon-smoked mackerel with a hot and sour green papaya salad

Serves 4 to 6

4 to 6 mackerel, weighing about 9 to 10½oz each
⅓ cup vegetable oil, for frying
flour

For the marinade
2 teaspoons soft brown sugar
2 tablespoons soy sauce
juice of 1 lime
freshly ground black pepper

For smoking
3½oz dry white Thai rice
2oz loose-leaf jasmine tea
2 lemongrass stems, coarsely chopped
1½in piece of ginger, peeled and cut into thin matchsticks
3 tablespoons soft brown sugar
3½oz dried coconut
4 star anise, broken
2 cinnamon sticks
1 tablespoon fennel seeds, crushed
1 tablespoon coriander seeds, crushed

Clean and gut the mackerel, removing the gills and the dark line of dried blood close to the spine along the top of the belly cavity. You can remove the head from the fish if desired. Wash the fish until the water runs clear, then pat dry with paper towels. Make three diagonal cuts down to the bone on each side of the fish.

Combine all the marinade ingredients in a bowl, then rub the marinade into the cuts in the fish. Line a large wok with two layers of tin foil. Mix together all the smoking ingredients and place them in the center of the wok. Set up a rack on top of the wok. Place the whole mackerel on top of the rack and cover with a lid. If you do not have a lid, use a large upturned metal bowl and seal the edges with crumpled tin foil.

Start the heat on medium to high so the smoking mix begins to caramelize. Smoke the fish for 10 minutes. Turn the mackerel once, then smoke for another 10 minutes. Remove from the heat and allow it to cool with the lid on, to contain all the smoke. When the fish has cooled, place in the fridge to firm up for 20 minutes.

Next make the salad. Peel the skin off the papaya or mangoes and slice the flesh into ribbons. Stack the ribbons of unripe fruit in small piles, and then finely slice into thin matchsticks.

Preheat the oven to 350°F. Place the raw peanuts on a baking sheet and bake in the oven until golden brown, about 4 minutes. Do not overcook them, as they become bitter when too dark. Place the chiles and garlic in a pestle and mortar with the salt and sugar and pound until you have a smooth paste. Add the lime and orange juices along with the fish sauce and vinegar. Taste the dressing: it should be hot, sweet, sour, and salty. If you prefer more heat, add some more chile.

For the hot and sour salad

- 2 medium-hard green papaya or 3 unripe mangoes
- 3½oz raw skinless peanuts
- 2 red chiles, seeded and finely chopped
- 1 garlic clove, green central stem discarded
- pinch of salt
- 1 teaspoon sugar
- 4 tablespoons fresh lime juice
- 2 tablespoons fresh orange juice
- 2 tablespoons fish sauce
- 1 tablespoon rice vinegar
- 1½in piece of fresh ginger, peeled and finely sliced into thin matchsticks
- 4 scallions, finely sliced
- 4 sprigs of fresh cilantro
- 3 sprigs of fresh mint

When ready to serve, place a wok or a large frying pan over medium to high heat. Add the oil and continue heating until the oil is hot. To check, drop a crumb or sliver of ginger into the hot oil; it should start to sizzle immediately. Meanwhile, remove the fish from the fridge, pat dry with paper towels, and dust with a little flour. Carefully add the mackerel one at a time to the hot oil (cook no more than 2 to 3 fish at a time). Cook for 2 minutes on each side so that the skin is crispy and golden brown. Carefully remove the fish with a slotted spoon and drain on paper towels. Allow the oil to get hot again and then repeat with the remaining fish.

Place the shredded papaya or mango in a large bowl with the ginger and scallions. Tear in the cilantro leaves and add the mint and half the roasted peanuts. Dress the salad with about two-thirds of the dressing. Crush the remaining peanuts and scatter them over the fish and papaya salad, then splash the remaining dressing over the smoked mackerel just before serving alongside the smoked mackerel.

TIP This is a simple way of transforming the flavor of a delicate fish. Other fish can be also be used; oily ones are best, such as mackerel, sardines, or salmon.

For the best results when cooking mackerel, it is best to keep it simple. This spice mix does just that and, combined with the firm pickled cucumbers, cuts through the fatty richness of the freshly cooked mackerel fillets.

fennel and peppered mackerel fillet with pickled cucumber salad

Serves 4 to 6

For the pickled cucumber salad
2 cucumbers, cut in half lengthwise and seeded
1 teaspoon salt
1 red chile, seeded and finely chopped
⅓ cup white wine vinegar
2 teaspoons sugar
juice of ½ lemon
1 tablespoon coriander seeds, crushed
4 star anise
2 bay leaves
3 scallions, finely chopped
4 sprigs of fresh mint

For the spice mix
3 teaspoons coriander seeds
2 teaspoons fennel seeds
½ teaspoon black peppercorns
1 teaspoon brown mustard seeds

4 to 6 mackerel fillets (1 per person)
salt

First make the pickled cucumber salad. Cut the cucumbers into 2½ x ¾in batons and place in a bowl, sprinkled with the salt. Mix together and leave for 30 minutes. Pour off any water that has accumulated from salting the cucumbers, lightly rinse under running water, and then pat dry with paper towels. Place the cucumber batons in a bowl with the chile.

Heat a saucepan over medium heat and add the vinegar, sugar, lemon juice, and the spices and bay leaves. Bring to a boil and mix together until the sugar is dissolved. Leave to cool. When the mixture is cool, add in the cucumbers and toss together. Leave to stand for 30 minutes to 2 hours. The longer you leave them, the softer the cucumbers will be.

To make the spice mix for the mackerel, coarsely grind the spices in a spice grinder or pestle and mortar. (Grinding whole spices yourself gives an enhanced aroma and adds texture.) Preheat the broiler. Lay the mackerel fillets on a baking sheet and season with salt, and then scatter the spice mix over the flesh. Broil until golden brown and cooked.

When ready to serve, add the scallions and mint to the cucumber salad and serve with the grilled mackerel fillets. This dish works well with a bottle of crisp Viognier or Semillon, as the citrus fruit qualities of the wine work wonderfully with the toasted spices and will cut through the richness of the mackerel.

In Istanbul, you get an amazing blend of cultures, with Europe on one side of the golden horn and Asia on the other. The layers of history and tradition in this magnificent city seem to exist in harmony, and the same is true of the food. A typical simple lunch by the bridge is fried mackerel in a bread roll with tomato and onion; it is tasty and fresh but not very sophisticated. However, there are much more elaborate dishes that have their roots in exotic spice bazaars of the East. I enjoyed these grilled mackerel in a less traveled part of town. The spices and the sourness of the lemon cut through the richness of the fresh mackerel beautifully.

turkish spice-grilled mackerel with lemon and bay leaves

Serves 4 to 6

6 fresh bay leaves
4 cardamom pods
salt and freshly ground black pepper
2 garlic cloves
2 small dried chiles
1 teaspoon ground allspice
¼ teaspoon freshly grated nutmeg
¼ teaspoon cayenne pepper
2 tablespoons olive oil
4 to 6 mackerel (allow 1 per person)
1 lemon, plus wedges to serve
6 sprigs of fresh flat-leaf parsley,
  coarsely chopped

Preheat a grill, broiler, or griddle pan to a high heat.

Coarsely chop the bay leaves and place in a pestle and mortar with the cardamom pods and 2 teaspoons of salt. Grind together until you are left with bright green powder. Push the mixture through a sieve into a bowl to remove any husks or pieces of stalk. This is bay leaf salt; it is delicious on its own and can be used to season roast potatoes or grilled meats or fish.

Crush together the garlic, dried chiles, and spices in a pestle and mortar and mix with the bay leaf salt. Add the olive oil.

Gut the mackerel and clean inside and out. Cut out the gills and remove any blood from the belly cavity. Pat the inside of the fish dry with paper towels. Rub most of the spice mix inside and outside of each fish.

Cut the lemon into quarters lengthwise, then chop each quarter into small triangular slices. Mix with the remaining spice marinade and season well with lots of black pepper. Finely chop the parsley and add to the mixture. Stuff the mackerel with the lemon and parsley, place them on the grill or griddle pan or under the broiler, and cook for 3 to 4 minutes on each side or until golden brown and crispy. Do not overcook smaller fish like mackerel, or they will dry out. Serve with wedges of lemon, a selection of salads and lots of fresh bread.

Mackerel was one of the first fish that I caught as a fisherman. My friend and I once landed 94 in an hour and a half! My mother arrived with a clean bin and we filled it to the brim—we were giving the fish away by the dozen to anyone we passed on the drive home. Mackerel is at its best when cooked incredibly fresh. Many people say they do not like mackerel because it is oily (that is the whole point of it!), but in this recipe the fish are coated in a hot and sour marinade of piquant horseradish, English mustard, and seasoned yogurt, which cuts through its fattiness. I often demonstrate this dish in a fish class for beginners, and get everyone to fillet the mackerel first.

grilled mackerel with horseradish, lemon, and mustard

Serves 4 to 6

2 tablespoons creamed horseradish
9oz Greek-style yogurt
salt and freshly ground black pepper
1 teaspoon hot English mustard,
    such as Colman's
grated zest and juice of 1 lemon
1 teaspoon red wine vinegar
3 sprigs of fresh flat-leaf parsley
4 to 6 mackerel (allow 1 per person)

Combine the horseradish and yogurt in a bowl. Season the mixture with salt and black pepper. Mix the mustard with the lemon juice and vinegar, and stir in the lemon zest. Add this mixture to the yogurt.

Coarsely chop the parsley and stir into the yogurt mixture. Taste the sauce: the mustard and horseradish should make it hot (it will lose a lot of its heat when cooked), the vinegar and lemon juice make it sour, and it should also be a little salty.

Preheat the broiler. Lay the mackerel fillets skin-side down on a baking sheet and spread with the horseradish, lemon, and mustard sauce. Place the fish under the broiler for 4 to 5 minutes until the sauce is caramelized on top and the fish is cooked. Serve as a starter with a mixed leaf salad.

The Spanish name of this recipe belies the roots of the dish. Escabeche refers to a method of pickling fish in spices that is used throughout the Spice Islands of the West Indies. Similar methods of preparing fish can be found in Mexico as well as in other Central American countries. The huge movement of people and the important trade in spices to England from the West Indies in the eighteenth century meant that this style of preparing fish became common in the English culinary repertoire of the time. Many of the eighteenth-century versions of escabeche are virtually identical to recipes still used in the Spice Islands and Central America today. The fish fillets or small steaks are lightly fried, then immersed in a spicy mixture with oil and wine vinegar, but are eaten cold. It makes an excellent starter for a summer lunch.

spiced mackerel escabeche

Serves 6

6 medium-sized mackerel, cleaned and
    gutted with heads removed
juice of 2 limes
2 teaspoons salt
10 black peppercorns
1 teaspoon coriander seeds
4 allspice berries
3 cloves
2 garlic cloves, crushed
1 cinnamon stick
4 fresh bay leaves
¾ cup white wine vinegar
1 teaspoon sugar
½ cup extra virgin olive oil
1 red onion, cut into wafer-thin slivers
2 medium-hot red chiles, seeded and
    finely chopped
large sprig of fresh thyme

Cut the fish on the diagonal into 1in slices, following the first cut behind the gills that was made to remove the head. Place the mackerel in a bowl. Mix the lime juice and half the salt in ¾ cup water and pour over the fish. Leave for 1 hour, turning the pieces a few times.

Place the peppercorns, coriander seeds, allspice, and cloves in a pestle and mortar or spice grinder and coarsely crush (a bit of texture is fine). Add the garlic and continue to crush to form a paste. Put the paste in a saucepan with the cinnamon stick, bay leaves, vinegar, sugar, and remaining salt. Bring the mixture to a boil. Add the extra virgin olive oil and ⅓ cup of water and bring up to a boil once more. Remove the pan from the heat.

Drain the fish and pat dry with paper towels. Heat a little oil in a heavy-bottomed pan over medium to high heat and lightly cook the fish slices for 3 minutes on each side until golden brown. Place the browned fish in one layer in a shallow serving dish. If they won't fit, don't make a second layer of fish; use two dishes instead. Pour the hot liquid over the fish and leave to marinate for 2 hours. (Marinating with hot liquid means the fish really absorbs all the amazing flavors.)

Half an hour before you are ready to serve the fish, carefully spoon off some of the liquid and put it into a bowl. Add the onion, chile, and thyme and leave to steep. This will soften the texture and intensify the flavor of the onion.

When ready to serve, scatter the onion and juice over the mackerel. Serve with lots of crusty bread and a crisp Chilean Sauvignon Blanc that has a hint of citrus on the palate. Alternatively serve with ice-cold Spanish or Mexican beer.

california tuna

Species: albacore tuna (*Thunnus alalunga*)
Certification: August 2007
Location: Pacific Ocean
Fishing methods: pole-and-line and troll-and-jig
Fishery tonnage: 5,000 metric tons
Vessels: members of the American Albacore Fisheries Association (AAFA)

california albacore tuna

Albacore tuna's potential was discovered almost by accident in 1903, when Alfred Halfhill, owner of one of San Diego's biggest canneries, found himself lacking enough sardines to keep his operations in full swing. He turned his attention to the albacore tuna and found it to be delicious. When the meat was steam cooked, it turned white, reminding Halfhill of cold chicken. His "Chicken of the Sea" became world famous. Thousands flocked to San Diego to find work in the booming new industry and the city was branded "tuna capital of the world." Then, almost all albacore was used for canning. Nowadays, some is still used for top-quality canned products, but most is smoked or cut into steaks to take full advantage of its superb flavor and high oil content. Many tuna stocks are now depleted and in danger. Buying blue fin has become unacceptable, and finding a sustainable yellow fin loin is hard work. Currently, American Albacore Fisheries Association (AAFA) albacore is the only tuna in the world certified as sustainable.

top right The harbor of Westport where boats from all kinds of small seafood companies drop their catch.

bottom right An AAFA fisherman enjoys a relaxing moment as the boat moves toward the rich fishing grounds.

Orca, Captain Larry

Larry is the skipper of a traditional 35-foot wooden tuna vessel named *Orca*. With his huge arms and loud voice, he is the stereotypical man of the sea. Larry does nothing without Jeff; they have been working together for more than 20 years and are ready for another trip catching albacore tuna on the rough North Pacific. "Only when our ship is full will we return," says Larry. "We take enough fuel with us to be at sea for at least 30 days." Unfortunately, the weather is a little too good for commercial fishing, with sun and a flat sea forecast. "I like to have the sea noisy because when it's calm the tuna hear my motor coming and run away," Larry explains. Ideally, there would be a northwesterly breeze of 10 to 15 knots.

An hour before sunrise on the second day, Larry and Jeff are waking up. Fortified by hot coffee and breakfast, they will be ready to fish as soon as the sun starts to rise. "We work 18 hours a day and don't quit till it is dark," says Larry. He first went fishing for tuna with his father when he was eight years old, but he has also had a spell in the Bering Sea, fishing for crab and pollack. "I was 18 when I bought my first boat but I've had the *Orca* for 12 years."

By early morning, the boat is 200 miles off the coast. Larry and Jeff are totally concentrated as they seek out the first tuna of the trip. When they fail to find a single fish during the first hour, they decide to try elsewhere. The catch starts in earnest when the *Orca* is 75 miles closer to the coast. Jeff takes the albacore off the hook, lands them on deck, and drains them. Then he "brings them to bed," as he refers to the process of brine freezing the fish. "The optimum temperature to

"When you see the fishermen, you cannot believe it is true that every single tuna is caught one at a time."

top left Every single tuna is caught individually by a pole and line. Two fishermen prepare their gear for the next trip.

bottom left The men at sea cook a hearty meal to energize themselves for the hard work of the coming catches.

top right A catch of albacore tuna is collected from on board a boat. Some tuna are frozen on board, but other boats land them on shore fresh.

keep them at is 7°F," he explains. "That way, we get the best possible quality." The forecast was right, the weather is a bit too calm, but enough fish has been caught to satisfy the two men.

At around 11:30pm they turn on the *Orca*'s radar alarm and head for bed, leaving the boat drifting easily on the tiny Pacific waves. In the middle of the night, a loud bell suddenly rings through the staff cabins. Larry wakes in fear and runs toward the steer house. It transpires that their boat has collided with another fishing vessel. The poll of the *Orca* has gone straight through the window adjacent to the other captain's steering wheel. Larry and Jeff erect bright lights to try to salvage the situation. After some time they conclude the damage is only slight, but they immediately start to repair the poll as it needs to be in full swing again by daybreak.

Larry is very happy to work for the AAFA. "They do things differently from other people in this business, securing stable prices and opening up European markets. We like them and will do everything we can to support them." Thanks to the MSC certificate and the marketing effort of Fishes, he gets a better price for his tuna. "I didn't know much about the MSC," he admits, "but I realize this is the way to go, for the seas, the fishermen, and the consumers."

After nearly two weeks at sea, the *Orca* comes back into Newport harbor with a total catch of 7,000 pounds They used to come back with 8,000 pounds, but for quality reasons they now limit their catch to 7,000 pounds. Bill, the plant manager on shore, gets 10 strong men to unload Larry and Jeff's tuna as Larry looks on proudly. When the boat is empty, they clean the deck and prepare for the next trip. They will be leaving again tomorrow.

Bountiful, Captain Tom Timmer

Tom is in his fifties and a very experienced fisherman; he started fishing for Dungeness crab and salmon during the 1970s and knows the Pacific extremely well. He is currently enjoying his third season with the AAFA. Like many other tuna fishermen, he was attracted to the association by its new approach to the market and the prospect of receiving stable prices.

"You catch albacore only when it's light. The days are as long as the sun is up."

Tom and his two-man crew wake up 45 minutes before sunrise without fail. While it is still dark, bright lights on the deck are used to attract small bait to the surface in the hope that the tuna will follow. It certainly seems to work: by the time we start fishing, there are plenty of albacore around. At this stage in the season, Tom and his crew use brightly colored plastic jigs to catch the tuna. "The fancy colors are to make the people happy," he explains. "The fish can only see in black and white." During the season, the catching method will change. Once the water temperature reaches 55 to 65°F, small fish like anchovies and sardines start to appear, increasing the density of the schools of tuna. At this stage it will be more effective to use the "pole and troll" technique. The fish will also be larger and more fatty due to the abundance of feed in the warmer waters and have one of the highest Omega-3 contents of any type of tuna.

The life of a fisherman is sometimes tough. Tom has twice survived his boat sinking. The first time he was crab fishing in winter. "The back deck of the boat took loads of water and it became too heavy. The weather was very rough. I told my crew to take the life raft while I made a mayday call. But things happened so quickly that I didn't get a return call. The crew made it to the life raft, but it drifted away, so I had no chance to join them. I was a good swimmer but it was hard to stay above the surface. I was getting really tired, and just when I was thinking this was about it, I heard an engine." The second time Tom sank was the result of a poorly designed boat. "It just rolled over," he recalls. On this occasion he did manage to get on to a life raft and was rescued by a colleague after six hours at sea.

Being a fisherman inevitably influences your personal life. "Spending 17 days in a row at sea and not coming home for months isn't easy," Tom confesses. "The hardest part is being away from your family. I hardly saw my kids growing up. None of them will go into fishing." Tom reveals that this is his last season with the albacore fishery. He has really enjoyed his life at sea but he has recently bought a vineyard and plans to continue his life on land. A year from now we hope to be sampling his new wines.

A few days after this interview we heard the tragic news that Tom had died in a car accident.

top left Three men setting out one of the nets employed to catch smaller fish that are used as bait to attract the tuna.

right The sequence of the tuna catch. Once caught, the tuna is dropped into a tank where it is frozen. When the boat lands on shore, the frozen albacore is taken out for production. The AAFA uses the best freezing techniques to preserve the quality of its product.

This is a deliciously rustic dish that spells hot summer. Seared tuna is served with a warm dressing made of roasted garlic cloves, cherry tomatoes, crushed black olives, rosemary, olive oil, and balsamic vinegar. The sweet roasted garlic makes a delicious contrast against the sour balsamic, tomatoes, and olives. The black pepper and arugula served with the tuna pieces give the dish a delicate heat.

tuna with roasted garlic and cherry tomatoes, rosemary, and black olives

Serves 4 to 6

30 cherry tomatoes, halved
12 garlic cloves
olive oil, for cooking
salt and freshly ground black pepper
20 to 30 black olives, pitted
2 sprigs of fresh rosemary
2 tablespoons balsamic vinegar
3 tablespoons extra virgin olive oil
1 fresh albacore tuna steak per person
arugula or mixed salad leaves, to serve

Preheat the oven to 350°F.

Place the halved tomatoes and garlic in a roasting pan with a little olive oil, salt, and black pepper. Add the olives and rosemary and toss gently to coat everything with the oil. Roast for 25 minutes. When the tomatoes are cooked, remove the pan from the oven and leave to rest for 5 minutes—this will allow the juices to be released to make the sauce; add the balsamic vinegar and extra virgin olive oil to the roasting pan to make a warm vinaigrette.

Heat some oil in a heavy-bottomed frying pan over medium to high heat. Season the tuna steaks with salt and black pepper. Do not overload the pan with cold fish, or the temperature will drop and the fish will boil rather than be seared; instead cook the fish in two or three batches. Sear the tuna in the frying pan for 1 minute, gently turn it over, and cook it for another minute for rare; if you prefer medium-rare, allow about another 20 seconds on each side, but no more. When removed from the pan, the fish will continue cooking from the residual heat and the salty, acidic marinade.

Remove the seared tuna from the pan and set aside. Scatter some arugula or mixed leaves over a large platter. Spoon half of the tomato mixture over the arugula and then arrange the seared tuna steaks on top. When you are ready to serve, spoon over the remaining tomato mixture with its warm juices. The tuna is meaty in taste and the tomatoes and garlic are rustic and robustly flavored, so I would suggest a light red wine such as a chilled Pinot Noir as an accompaniment.

TIP This dish looks great served on a platter in the middle of the table, or if you prefer, you could plate the tuna individually. If you don't have any rosemary, use sprigs of thyme or marjoram—all these herbs work well with the combined flavors of the tomatoes, garlic, and olives.

Marinating the tuna in turmeric, crushed garlic, and chile means the fish takes on lots of color and flavor to create a very striking dish. The fish can be grilled rare as a steak or as cubes that can be served as a canapé.

seared tuna with fresh turmeric, scallion, and chile

Serves 4 to 6

½ small bunch of cilantro, stems and roots reserved
2 garlic cloves, peeled
1½in piece of ginger, peeled and finely sliced
salt and freshly ground black pepper
2 medium-hot red chiles, seeded and finely chopped
1½in piece of turmeric root, peeled, or 1 teaspoon ground turmeric (see Tip)
2 tablespoons hot water
1¾ to 2½lb albacore tuna (if you can, buy the tuna in one piece, then cut it into slices weighing about 6 to 8oz, allowing 1 steak per person)
juice of 2 limes
2 tablespoons soy sauce
olive oil, for cooking
4 scallions, green parts cut into 1¼in lengths, cut in half lengthwise and cut into thin strands
20 snow peas, ends trimmed and cut into thin strands

Finely chop the cilantro roots and stems with the garlic and ginger. Place in a pestle and mortar with a pinch of salt. Pound the mixture into a coarse paste. Add the chiles and continue to work into a paste. Peel the flesh of the turmeric into thin slivers (note that fresh turmeric is a very strong dye; if you do not want to dye your hands and everything that you touch bright orange, use it carefully and wear rubber gloves). Place the slivers in a shallow metal bowl. Add the hot water and the spice paste: this will form the marinade.

Season the tuna steaks with black pepper (no salt at this stage as the fish needs to marinate). Place the tuna in the shallow bowl with the marinade, cover, and set aside for 30 minutes. Turn the steaks and baste with the marinade a number of times throughout the time.

Heat a large heavy-bottomed frying pan over medium to high heat. Remove the fish from the marinade and gently shake off the excess. Pat the fillets dry with paper towels. Add the lime juice and soy sauce to the marinade. Season the tuna steaks with a little salt. Do not over season the fish, because soy sauce is salty.

Do not overload the pan with cold fish or the temperature will drop and the fish will boil rather than be seared; instead cook it in two or three batches. Add a little oil to the pan and sear the tuna for 1 minute, then gently turn it over and cook for another minute for rare; if you prefer medium-rare, allow about another 20 seconds on each side. When removed from the pan, the fish will continue cooking from the residual heat and the salty, acidic marinade.

Remove the tuna from the pan and return it to the shallow bowl with the soy, turmeric, and lime juice dressing. Spoon the dressing over the fish and add the shredded scallions, snow peas, and half the cilantro leaves.

Serve the tuna and shredded vegetables on individual plates or on a central platter for the table. Garnish with the remaining cilantro leaves.

TIP Fresh turmeric is available from most Asian grocers and Chinese and Thai speciality stores. Its fresh vivid orange color looks amazing when it is shaved into thin slivers.

The salsa for this dish works well with many types of fish. It is made with raw fennel, preserved lemon, herbs, red chile, oil, and lemon juice. Half of the fennel is puréed with a little oil and the other half is finely chopped to provide some texture to the salsa. The fennel, parsley, and mint make a delicious combination that complements the sweetness of the seared fish.

seared fillet of albacore tuna with fennel and lemon salsa

Serves 4 to 6

For the salsa
3 lemons
3 tablespoons coarse rock salt
1 red chile, seeded and finely chopped
6 tablespoons extra virgin olive oil
2 fennel bulbs, trimmed and diced
   (reserve the fine fennel herb fronds)
salt and freshly ground black pepper
3 sprigs of fresh parsley, finely chopped
3 sprigs of fresh mint, finely chopped

1 piece of albacore tuna, weighing about
   2 to 2¾lb
olive oil, for cooking
mixed peppery greens such as arugula,
   watercress, and mustard leaves,
   to serve

First, make the salsa. Place two of the lemons in a small saucepan with the rock salt. Cover with cold water and bring to a boil, then cook until soft when pierced with the tip of a sharp knife, about 10 to 12 minutes. When the lemons are cooked, refresh them under cold water. Halve and remove all the insides and pith with a sharp knife. Trim down the lemon skin from the inside, so you are just left with lozenges of lemon zest. If you cover the lozenges at this stage with olive oil, you will have preserved lemon zest; it will keep covered in the fridge for up to 6 weeks.

Finely chop the preserved lemon and mix with the red chile. Add the juice of the remaining fresh lemon and mix with the olive oil. Place half the diced fennel in a food processor with a little of the oil to make a purée. Mix all the fennel together with the lemon and chile mixture. Season well with freshly ground black pepper and then salt. Do not add the chopped herbs until you are ready to serve, because acid will cook the herbs and turn them black.

Heat a heavy-bottomed frying pan or griddle pan. Cut the piece of tuna in half lengthwise along the grain. Then cut these pieces in half lengthwise, resulting in four pieces with a 2-inch diameter. Rub the pieces with a little oil and season well with salt and freshly ground black pepper.

Place the pieces of tuna in the hot pan, starting furthest away from you. Sear the tuna until the flesh is golden brown, about 1 to 1½ minutes. With a pair of tongs, roll the piece of tuna 90° toward you and sear the next side. Repeat until all the sides are golden brown. Remove from the heat and wrap each piece very tightly in plastic wrap and place in the freezer for 20 to 25 minutes to firm up the flesh and make it easier to cut into thin slices.

Unwrap the tuna, and with a thin sharp knife, cut thin slices across the grain. Use a light pressure, as if you are cutting a loaf of bread, and try and cut the tuna as thinly as possible. Each slice will have a thin cooked perimeter.

Add the chopped herbs to the salsa and check the seasoning. Dress the arugula and mixed peppery leaves with some olive oil and a little salsa. Spoon the salsa over the slices of tuna and serve.

This classic Mexican coastal salsa could be served with many types of fish, but it is particularly good with tuna as the acidity, salt, and peppery heat of the sauce cut the sweet richness of the fish. The deep continental waters of the Pacific Ocean have been home to schools of tuna since they evolved, and these beans, chiles, and tomatoes also began their culinary evolution on the continent of South America, so variations of this dish have been made for hundreds, if not thousands, of years.

albacore tuna with white beans and mexican green salsa

Serves 4 to 6

For the white beans

3½oz dried cannellini beans, soaked overnight in cold water
2 bay leaves
1 celery rib
3 tablespoons olive oil
1 garlic clove, finely chopped
1 tablespoon red wine vinegar
juice of 1 lemon
3 sprigs of fresh parsley, chopped
salt and freshly ground black pepper

For the green salsa

1lb green tomatoes
4 green serrano chiles, seeded and finely chopped
1 medium-sized onion, finely chopped
6 scallions, finely chopped
½ medium-sized bunch of fresh flat-leaf parsley
½ medium-sized bunch of cilantro
¼ cup olive oil
4 garlic cloves, finely chopped
juice of 2 limes

2 to 2¾lb albacore tuna, cut into thick steaks
olive oil, for cooking
1 teaspoon cumin seeds, crushed

Drain the soaked beans and place them in a saucepan. Cover with cold water and add the bay leaves and celery. Bring to a boil, then simmer, using a ladle to skim off any foam that rises to the surface. Simmer for 1 hour, until the beans are soft and tender. Remove them from the heat and allow to cool in their own liquid. Discard the bay leaves and the celery.

Meanwhile, make the green salsa. Cut the tomatoes in half and grate over a large bowl. The skin will stay in your palm; discard it. Place the chiles, onion, and tomatoes in a food processor and blend to a paste. Add the scallions, parsley, and half of the cilantro (reserving half of the leaves to finish the salsa), then blend again to a smooth paste. Heat the olive oil in a heavy-bottomed pan over medium to high heat. Add the garlic and cook for 2 minutes until pale golden and fragrant. Add the salsa and season well with salt and black pepper. Cook over medium heat for about 10 to 15 minutes until the sauce has began to thicken. Remove from the heat and add the lime juice and remaining cilantro. Taste and adjust the seasoning.

To finish the beans, heat the olive oil in a saucepan and cook the garlic until golden and aromatic, about 1 to 2 minutes. Add the cooked beans and about ⅓ cup of their cooking liquid. Bring to a boil and cook until the beans are hot. Add the vinegar, lemon juice, and parsley. Season the beans well with salt and black pepper. Set aside.

Preheat a heavy-bottomed frying pan or griddle pan over medium to high heat. Rub the tuna with a little oil so that the seasoning will stick to it. Season well with salt, black pepper, and the crushed cumin seeds. When the pan is hot, add a little oil and sear the tuna until the flesh is golden brown, about 1½ to 2 minutes. Using tongs, turn the fish and sear the other side. Remove from the heat. Cut the tuna steaks across the grain into five slices.

Spoon some beans onto the center of plates or a large platter and fan out the slices of tuna on top. Spoon over some of the green salsa just before serving. If you like, you could serve this dish with some mixed peppery greens alongside, such as arugula or watercress.

Chermoula is a fiery North African spice paste made from coriander seeds, chile, garlic, and lemon. It comes in many forms: from pastes and marinades to colorful salsas where tomatoes and chopped roasted peppers are added. In this version, inspired by one created by Diana Henry in her beautiful book *Crazy Water, Pickled Lemons*, small steaks of fresh tuna are marinated in a chermoula paste and then quickly fried. Serve these stunning pieces of fish around a jeweled and textured mound of couscous studded with pomegranate seeds, sour cherries, and cranberries. Together these exotic and inviting dishes are like a brightly colored eastern mosaic, with many sumptuous shades.

chermoula-marinated tuna

Serves 6 to 8

1 albacore tuna steak per person

For the chermoula
3 teaspoons coriander seeds
3 teaspoons cumin seeds
3 teaspoons ground cinnamon
1 teaspoon paprika
2 garlic cloves, halved
1 chile, seeded and finely chopped
¼ cup olive oil, plus extra for cooking
grated zest and juice of 1 lemon
1 bunch of cilantro, chopped
½ bunch of fresh flat-leaf parsley, chopped

In a pestle and mortar, grind the coriander and cumin seeds, then add the cinnamon and paprika. Add the garlic and chile and continue to work until you have a smooth paste.

Add the olive oil, lemon juice and zest, cilantro, and parsley to the mixture. Pour the mixture over the tuna steaks and leave to marinate for 30 minutes before cooking.

Heat a little oil in a heavy-bottomed pan and, just before cooking, season the fish steaks with salt and freshly ground black pepper. Do not overload the pan with cold fish, or the temperature will drop and the fish will boil rather than be seared; instead, cook the fish in two or three batches. Sear the tuna for 1 minute, then gently turn it over and cook for another minute for rare; if you prefer medium-rare, allow about another 20 seconds on each side, but no more. When removed from the pan, the fish will continue cooking from the residual heat and the salty, acidic marinade.

Serve the steaks on a large platter with the jeweled pomegranate couscous (*see* opposite) in the center.

This marinade can be used for meaty fish such as tuna, or also for chicken, lamb, or beef. You can make the chermoula more substantial by adding some chopped roasted peppers and chopped cherry tomatoes. In this form, it becomes part of the substance of the dish and could also be used for grilled squid or shrimp.

pomegranate couscous with mint and roasted almonds

Serves 6 to 8

10½oz couscous
grated zest and juice of 1 lemon
grated zest and juice of 1 orange
1 tablespoon red wine vinegar
2 tablespoons pomegranate molasses
3 tablespoons olive oil
2 tablespoons sesame oil
3 tablespoons dried sour cherries
3 tablespoons dried cranberries
½ chile, seeded and finely chopped
salt and freshly ground black pepper
½ teaspoon ground cinnamon
½ cup blanched skinless almonds,
   pistachio nuts, or pine nuts
½ cup sesame seeds
4 scallions
30 fresh mint leaves
20 fresh parsley or basil leaves
1 bunch of arugula
2 pomegranates

Combine the couscous, lemon and orange juices, and zests in a large bowl. Pour 1¾ cups of boiling water into a jug; mix in the vinegar, pomegranate molasses, and the two oils. Add the sour cherries, cranberries, and chile to the couscous. Pour the water mixture over the couscous and gently stir to combine. Season with salt and black pepper and cinnamon and cover the bowl with plastic wrap, sealing the edges; leave for 5 minutes. As the couscous soaks up the hot liquid, it will absorb all the strong aromatic flavors.

After 5 minutes, remove the plastic wrap and stir the couscous with a fork to break up any lumps or clumps that have stuck together.

Dry-roast the nuts and sesame seeds until they are golden brown. Trim the scallions and finely slice. Coarsely chop the herbs and arugula. Mix all these ingredients with the couscous.

To prepare the pomegranates, tap the fruits firmly with a wooden spoon all over. Cut them in half—it will create a lot of juice. Hold the fruit cut-side down in one hand and continue to tap the outside firmly with the wooden spoon. All the seeds will fall out, leaving the bitter white pith behind. Mix the seeds with the couscous, reserving some to use as a garnish.

Taste the couscous and add more olive oil, lemon juice, or seasoning, if necessary. Serve sprinkled with the reserved pomegranate seeds.

This is a delicious fish carpaccio, which is simple to make and looks fancy too. The flavors of toasted, crushed fennel seeds, chiles, and lemon intermingle on the thin slivers of raw fish. All it needs is a liberal seasoning of sea salt and freshly cracked black pepper and a good splash of lemon and oil dressing, then every element of taste is represented for the tongue in its simplest form.

carpaccio of tuna with fennel seed, chile, and lemon

Serves 4 to 6

1lb 10oz albacore tuna (as 1 large fillet)
1 tablespoon fennel seeds
2 red chiles, halved and seeded
zest and juice of 1 lemon
4 tablespoons good-quality extra virgin olive oil
sea salt and freshly ground black pepper
3 sprigs of fresh dill or chervil, coarsely chopped

Slice the tuna as thinly as possible. Lay out a large piece of plastic wrap in double thickness. Place the slices of fish on the plastic wrap, cover with another double layer of plastic wrap, and gently tap the slices of fish with a rolling pin to flatten them further.

Lay the thin slivers of tuna on individual plates or on a large platter or board. In a dry frying pan, gently toast the fennel seeds until fragrant and aromatic, about 2 minutes. Place the fennel seeds in a pestle and mortar and coarsely crush so that they still have some texture and have released their aroma.

Take the chiles and lay them on a cutting board, skin-side down. (This makes them easier to chop because the inside flesh is softer.) Finely slice into thin half-moon slivers. Thinly pare the lemon zest and cut it into fine strips. Squeeze the lemon and mix the juice with the olive oil.

Scatter the toasted fennel seeds over the tuna slices. Repeat the process with the red chile slivers and the lemon zest strips. Season the fish with salt and black pepper.

When ready to serve, spoon some of the oil and lemon dressing over the top of the fish and scatter with the dill or chervil. Serve with a simple salad of arugula leaves and some lovely fresh bread, accompanied by a crisp fragrant white wine with a good combination of acidity and ripe fruit. I would recommend a Viognier or Pinot Gris as they will highlight the toasted fennel seeds and fresh herbs.

This is a very simple dish that needs little preparation. It looks very impressive, though—the crusted fish takes on a textured appearance from the sesame seeds, cinnamon, and coriander seeds, while the fresh green of the vegetables is punctuated with the red chile, and it all glistens with the zesty and spicy warm Asian vinaigrette.

spice-and-sesame-crusted tuna with stir-fried asparagus and zucchini and warm asian vinaigrette

Serves 4

For the Asian vinaigrette
grated zest and juice of 1 orange
½ tablespoon grated fresh ginger
2 scallions, finely sliced
½ teaspoon Schichimi Togarashi (Japanese seven-spice)
½ teaspoon sugar
salt and freshly ground black pepper
1 tablespoon soy sauce
2 tablespoons sesame oil
1 tablespoons vegetable oil (or peanut or olive oil)
1 tablespoon rice wine vinegar
juice of 1 lemon

2 to 2¾lb albacore tuna, in 1 large piece
2 teaspoons ground cinnamon
1 tablespoon crushed coriander seeds
3 tablespoons sesame seeds
olive oil, for cooking

For the wok-fried greens
1 garlic clove, finely chopped
1 red chile, seeded and finely chopped
½ tablespoon grated fresh ginger
bunch of thin-stemmed asparagus, cut into 1¼in lengths
4 medium-sized zucchini, cut into 1¼in lengths and then into batons the same size as the asparagus
large handful of snap peas
3 sprigs of fresh mint, coarsely torn

First make the vinaigrette. Mix together the orange zest and ginger, the scallions, Japanese seven-spice, and the sugar. Add all the other ingredients. Taste and adjust the flavorings as necessary: the dressing should be hot, sweet, salty, and sour. (You could add a little fresh chile, if desired.) This dressing can be made in advance and kept for a few days, but do taste before using and adjust the seasoning accordingly.

Cut the tuna into steaks and season with salt, black pepper, cinnamon, coriander seeds, and sesame seeds. Shake off the excess powder. Preheat a frying pan until hot. Add 1 tablespoon of olive oil, add the tuna steaks, and cook for 1½ minutes on each side. Remove from the heat and cut into three or four slices.

You should cook the greens at the same time as the tuna, because they will not take long, and it is important not to overcook the tuna. Heat a wok over medium to high heat. Add a splash of oil, then add the garlic, chile, and ginger. Cook for 1 minute, then add the asparagus, zucchini, and snap peas and cook for another 2 to 3 minutes. (If you prefer, you could use bok choy, spinach, or tender-stemmed broccoli.)

When the green vegetables are cooked, add some of the torn fresh mint. Season with salt and freshly ground black pepper. While the vegetables are cooking, warm through the Asian vinaigrette. Serve the sliced tuna on top of the wok-fried vegetables immediately. Dress with the warm Asian dressing and garnish with the remaining mint.

TIP Japanese seven-spice Schichimi Togarashi is a delicious blend of seven flavors: dried chile pepper, Sansho pepper (which is similar to Szechuan pepper), orange zest blended with black and white sesame seeds, poppy seeds, nori seaweed, and ginger. It is available in most Asian grocers and Chinese and Japanese speciality markets.

norway cod & haddock

Species: cod (*Gadus morhua*) and haddock (*Melanogrammus aeglefinus*)
Certification: February 2009
Location: along the northern Norwegian coast, covering regions
    including the spawning grounds of the Lofoten islands, the southern
    part of the Barents Sea, and the Svalbard area
Fishing methods: longline
Fishery tonnage: 5,000 metric tons of each species
Vessels: 10
Number of fisheries: 1

norway cod & haddock

The journey along the picturesque wind-swept fjord was spectacular, with sun on one side of the ferry and stormy weather on the other. The sheer scale of the landscape could be appreciated only when you saw a miniscule bus or truck driving along the shoreline. We were traveling to Måløy on the northwest Norwegian coast, home to Rolf Domstein and his brothers and headquarters of the family fishing business. Rolf's grandfather founded the business in 1929 as a fish-packing concern and it has been evolving and diversifying ever since.

Like many of his core team, Rolf was brought up in Måløy, left to complete his higher education, and then returned to put the knowledge he had acquired into practice. He is integrity personified. When fixed with his icy blue eyes, you are captivated and fall on every word he says. "My family has been in the fish business for three generations," says Rolf. "I hope it will be around in another three, but for that to happen the business must be sustainable."

Domstein Longline Partners is a co-op between Rolf Domstein and Ervik Havfiske, the leading longline fishing company in Norway. Longline fishing is selective because the bait, hook size, and line depth are specifically calculated to target the big cod and haddock. The smaller fish that are yet to spawn swim at a different level and so are not affected. Domstein fishes at least 13 miles out to sea to avoid catching coastal cod, which is not MSC-certified, and the by-catch is very small. Fishing is also primarily undertaken at night, significantly reducing the potential for seabirds to be caught up in equipment. According to John Eric Halnes, general manager of the Måløy fishery, these enlightened practices are nothing new in Norway. "We started fishery management long before any other country thought that it was important," he emphasizes. There are stern quotas and harsh penalties for miscreants who catch "black" fish. Domstein issues a guarantee of sustainability on each packet of fish that carries its brand. The guarantee has three pillars. First, Domstein fish are bought only from sustainable fisheries, as the firm's MSC certification testifies. Second, the company buys only longlined fish and only from vessels in its own fleet. The website features maps that show where the fish were caught and the quota status of each vessel. Domstein has also calculated the carbon footprint of its boats and factory. "We have full traceability on each box of fish, with the name of the boat and the catching area of the fish." Finally, all processing is carried out in Norway. This third point is very important to the local economy. As Rolf says, "this is the only way that people can live on the coast of Norway. It is the local community that maintains the sustainability of the fishery. The workers are the direct link from the sustainable product to the community."

top right The Norwegian flag in a blaze of glory en route to the Domstein fishery in Måløy. The extraordinary contrast of the journey's sunshine and storm clouds matches the contrasting image we have of sustainability and the highly technical approach that Domstein has adopted to achieve this.

bottom right The picturesque view of the longlining boat in the sunlit fjord is a far cry from what faces the young crew heading out to fish below the Artic Circle for the next seven weeks.

"We are fishmongers dealing with local business, but the market is all over the world."

top left The tough young crew relaxes with a bottomless pot of black coffee. When out at sea, these boys work harder than you could imagine possible.

bottom left A veteran in the Norwegian cod fishing business shows one of his young colleagues the tricks of the trade. The extraordinary indelible calligraphy of fresh haddock, with its distinctive "inked" black line running from head to tail.

top right 30,000 hooks primed and ready to shoot into the North Sea. They target the large mature cod and haddock that are certified as sustainable as these fish swim deeper than the juveniles and have already spawned at least twice.

In the 1940s and 50s there were huge herring fisheries in the area, but dependency on the species led to the collapse of the industry in the early 60s, whereupon fishing for herring was banned. The community survived by developing new technologies and markets. The fishery is going through a similar metamorphosis today. Filleting is now done by sophisticated machines, as labor costs in Norway are sky high. The fish is frozen at sea within half an hour of catching, which ensures that there is no time for rigor mortis to set in. This means that the freshness is trapped in the flesh. Domstein has also pioneered low-temperature defrosting techniques that allow the fish to be processed quickly but with no loss of quality. As a result, "the refreshed product is superior to much of the fresh fillet available on the market."

Aside from providing the MSC-certified cod and haddock, the fishery plays a central role in the life of the Måløy community. "We try to support the local cultural life and activities to make it more attractive for people to live here—particularly young people." Sales manager Øyvind Reed is the captain of the semi-professional local soccer team sponsored by Domstein. The company has also kept the local brass band in operation and many local events are supported by Rolf and his visionary team.

Domstein could have exploited its MSC certification to charge higher prices, but instead they just use it to sell more fish. Øyvind and his sales team have been working hard to promote their products around Europe and their approach is bearing fruit. The original certification was for ten longliner boats, but this is likely to increase to 17 to meet demand both in Norway and abroad. As Rolf says, "The sales of MSC-certified fish have surpassed all expectations. Swedish sales of cod and haddock fillets have increased by more than 50 percent since we started eco-labeling. Sales development in England, Holland, and Switzerland has also been very positive." All in all, Domstein is a trailblazing company and a great example to other fisheries.

A *bourride* is a spectacular rustic French stew of fresh and salted fish, which is then thickened with aïoli. Traditionally, bacalao (dried cod) is used, but in this recipe I think the fish should be freshly and more lightly salted. This is a dish that should be eaten outside with your sleeves rolled up, accompanied by some chilled wine, lots of fresh crusty bread—and some good friends.

bourride of salt cod with saffron aïoli

Serves 4 to 6

4 (7-ounce) pieces of Atlantic cod
4 heaping tablespoons coarse rock salt
1 tablespoon olive oil
5 garlic cloves, 4 finely chopped and
   1 left whole for the bread
2 large onions, finely chopped
1 leek, cleaned and coarsely chopped
3 sprigs of fresh parsley, leaves reserved
   for the garnish
2 bay leaves
1 sprig of fresh thyme
3 strips of orange zest
1¾ cups fish stock (see page 84)
1lb potatoes, peeled and cut into
   ¼in slices
1 French baguette, cut into slices

For the saffron aïoli
1 tablespoon boiling water
large pinch of saffron threads
3 garlic cloves
salt and freshly ground black pepper
2 egg yolks
1 teaspoon Dijon mustard
1 teaspoon red wine vinegar
1 cup extra virgin olive oil
juice of ½ lemon

Place 2 of the pieces of cod in a bowl and cover with the rock salt. (The salt must be coarse; if it is too fine it will be absorbed into the flesh too quickly.) Cut the remaining 2 pieces of cod into ¾in thick slices and chill until needed.

While the fish is salting, make the aïoli. Pour the boiling water over the saffron threads in a bowl and allow to infuse. Crush the garlic with a little salt until you have a smooth paste. Place the crushed garlic in a bowl and add the egg yolks, mustard, and vinegar. Using a wooden spoon, stir to combine the ingredients. Pour in the oil, drip by drip, stirring all the time to make a mayonnaise. Continue stirring until all the oil is used up and you have a thick emulsion. Add the saffron, its soaking liquid, and the lemon juice and stir to combine. Taste and adjust the seasoning.

After 1 hour, remove the fish from the salt, place in a colander in the sink, and run under cold water for 10 minutes. Make sure all the salt is washed off. The cod will be much firmer in texture now, and the color opaque and lighter. Cut the salted cod into ¾in thick slices.

Heat the oil in a deep saucepan. Add the chopped garlic and cook over low heat for 2 minutes until fragrant but without too much color. Add the onions and leek and cook for 3 minutes. Make a bouquet garni with the parsley stems, bay, and thyme and add to the vegetables with the orange zest. In a separate pan, bring the stock to a boil, then add the potatoes and simmer for 8 minutes. Add the slices of salted and fresh fish and poach for 5 minutes.

Transfer the fish and potatoes to a warm serving dish. Strain the cooking liquid through a sieve into a clean saucepan. Using a wooden spoon, press the vegetables against the side of the sieve to extract all their essences. Place the aïoli in a bowl and gently whisk 1 cup of the strained fish stock into the mixture to combine. Return this thickened mixture to the stock, whisking together so that it is combined. Return the pan to low heat and, using a wooden spoon, stir continuously until the soup thickens slightly. Gently pour the thickened soup over the fish and potatoes.

Toast the slices of bread and rub each one with a little garlic. Coarsely chop the reserved parsley leaves and scatter over the stew. Serve the bourride in large bowls with the toasted baguette.

This classic dish is simple yet effective, combining firm-fleshed fish with a fresh crunchy crust made from finely chopped herbs. It looks as good as it tastes; the bright colors make a delicious contrast with the rich milky color of the cod. If you don't want mashed potatoes, it is equally delicious served with lentils.

roast herb-crusted cod and mashed potatoes
with scallions and rosemary

Serves 4

For the herb crust
**1 thick slice of crusty bread, white
  or brown, crusts removed**
4 sprigs of fresh parsley
2 sprigs of fresh mint
small handful of arugula
grated zest of 1 lemon
**4 garlic cloves, roasted in their skins
  until soft**
¼ teaspoon cayenne pepper
salt and freshly ground black pepper
3 tablespoons olive oil

**4 pieces of cod fillet, weighing about
  7oz each, skin on**
olive oil, for cooking

For the mashed potatoes
**3¼lb potatoes, peeled and cut into
  equal-sized chunks**
3 tablespoons butter
⅓ cup milk
⅓ cup heavy cream
4 scallions, finely chopped
**1 large sprig of fresh rosemary, finely
  chopped**

First make the herb crust. Place all the ingredients except the oil into a food processor, process, and then, with the motor running slowly, add the oil to make a green paste.

Take the pieces of fish and spread about 2 tablespoons of the herb paste on to the skin side of each fillet. This can be done up to a couple of hours before cooking as long as you keep the fish refrigerated.

Next make the mashed potatoes. Cook the potatoes in boiling salted water until soft, drain, and put them through a potato ricer or mash well with a masher. In a small saucepan, bring the butter, milk, and heavy cream to a boil. Add the scallions and rosemary, season well with salt and black pepper, and simmer to infuse the flavors into the cream. Stir the cream and scallion mixture into the potatoes. Mix together and adjust the seasoning to suit your taste. Mashed potatoes can take lots of freshly ground black pepper.

Preheat the oven to 400°F. When ready to cook the fish, heat an ovenproof frying pan over medium to high heat. Season the pieces of fish with salt and black pepper. Add a splash of oil to the pan, then add the crusted cod fillets, skin-side up. Cook the fish for about 1 minute, then transfer the pan to the oven and roast for 10 to 12 minutes, depending on the thickness of the cod. Do not overcook the fish: remember that when it comes out of the oven, it maintains its heat and continues cooking. Serve the roasted fillet of cod with the hot mashed potatoes and some greens, accompanied by a chilled Sauvignon Blanc with crisp herbaceous qualities (see Tip).

TIP This dish would go very well with some simply braised spinach or grilled or roasted asparagus. It is important to have some texture to the green vegetables you choose, as a contrast to the soft potatoes.

This is a fantastic Royal Thai curry. All the flavors of hot, sweet, salty, and sour are represented, but the curry is predominantly hot from the chile and sour from the tamarind, lime juice, and lemongrass. The fish fillets are first grilled until rare to give them a great texture, flavor, and look, then cooked through in the curry sauce. It is a spectacular-looking dish, with a great contrast of colors among the white fish, yellow turmeric-stained curry, and the fresh green of the asparagus and herbs.

hot and sour curry of grilled cod
and asparagus

Serves 4 to 6

For the curry paste

4 stems lemongrass, tough outer leaves
    discarded and finely chopped
1½in piece of fresh galangal or ginger,
    peeled and finely chopped
4 garlic cloves
5 red chiles, seeded and finely
    chopped
6 cilantro roots, cleaned and
    chopped
1 teaspoon salt
2 red onions, coarsely chopped
1 red bell pepper, coarsely chopped

vegetable or olive oil, for cooking
2 teaspoons ground turmeric
4 kaffir lime leaves, plus 3 to garnish
2 lemongrass stems, tough outer leaves
    discarded
1 red chile, seeded
1lb cod fillet
salt and freshly ground black pepper
2 (14-ounce) cans coconut cream
juice of 2 limes
2 tablespoons tamarind pulp
2 tablespoons fish sauce
1 bunch of asparagus, cut into
    1¼in lengths
½ small bunch of cilantro, chopped

First make the curry paste. Starting with the lemongrass and galangal, purée all the ingredients except the onions and red pepper in a food processor. Once the consistency is smooth, add the onions and red pepper with a little water to help bring the mixture together into a paste.

Heat 1 tablespoon of oil in a heavy-bottomed pan over medium to high heat. Add the curry paste and cook slowly, stirring regularly to keep it from sticking. Add the ground turmeric and the 4 lime leaves. Cook until aromatic and fragrant, about 30 minutes. At this stage you should be able to smell the lemongrass and galangal in the curry paste; they are the hardest ingredients with the least water, so will cook last. If the paste sticks while cooking, add a little water to loosen it.

Before you start cooking the fish, finely chop the lemongrass and the red chile. Take the 3 lime leaves reserved for the garnish and turn them over so that the raised underside of the stem is uppermost. Shave off the raised stem with a sharp knife. Roll the leaves into a tight cigar shape. With a swift rolling motion, chop the lime leaves into thin needle-thread slivers. Set aside.

Preheat a griddle pan. Lightly oil the fish and season the fish with salt and black pepper and cook for 2 minutes on each side to bar-mark the fish. You are not cooking the fish all the way through, just searing it on the outside. Break the fish into large pieces.

Add the coconut cream to the curry paste and simmer to reduce by half. Add the lime juice, tamarind pulp, and the fish sauce; taste and adjust the seasoning. When the curry has reduced by half, add the grilled fish and the asparagus and poach gently over low heat for 5 minutes. Add half the chopped lemongrass, red chile, and lime leaves to the curry and mix together. Scatter the remaining garnish and cilantro over the finished curry before serving.

TIP You can use any type of sustainable fish for this curry, and you could also add green beans or potatoes to bulk it out.

One evening while I was visiting the Domstein cod fishery, Rolf Domstein invited us to dinner. Little did I know that I was going to be served the simplest and probably one of the most delicious pieces of fish that I have ever eaten. It is certainly in the top ten. Loins of cod, 2in thick, that had been alive and swimming only four hours before, awaited us. Exactly three times the weight of the fish was measured out in water and brought to a boil. A handful of salt (not a pinch) was added, and when the water boiled, the pan was removed from the heat and set aside. The fish was then lowered in and the lid replaced. In my eyes, it was not looking promising. Rolf proved me completely mistaken, however. The fish was poached in the cooling liquid before being served with steamed potatoes and carrots and melted salted butter poured over the top. There you have it—so simple and perfect. The key was the freshest fish, organic potatoes recently dug up, and delicious locally made butter. If you can guarantee all of these factors, give this dish a try. If you cannot trace the provenance of all the simple components, make this delicious fish pie instead.

norwegian fish pie

Serves 4 to 6

2¼lb fresh cod loin, skinned and
    pin-boned
3 quarts water
salt and freshly ground black pepper
2 tablespoons butter, plus extra for
    greasing
2 onions, finely chopped
3 tablespoons all-purpose flour
2 eggs, separated
1¾ cups milk
1 bay leaf
pinch of paprika
3 sprigs of fresh parsley, chopped
2 slices of white bread
¾ cup cheese, such as Cheddar
    or Jarlsberg, grated

Choose cod loins that are the same thickness, so they need the same amount of time to poach. Bring the water to a boil in a large pan and add 3 tablespoons salt. Once boiling, remove from the heat. Add the cod and cover with a lid. Poach for 10 minutes, then remove from the water with a slotted spoon.

Meanwhile, melt the butter in a pan over medium heat. Add the onions and cook until soft, about 8 minutes. Add the flour and stir with a wooden spoon until it is all combined. Cook the flour mixture, stirring to keep it from sticking, for another 4 minutes.

Stir the egg yolks into the roux using a wooden spoon. Add the milk a spoonful at a time, stirring constantly to avoid lumps. (You are making a béchamel sauce that has been made richer with the addition of the egg yolks.) Add the bay leaf and paprika. Taste the sauce and season with salt and black pepper if necessary.

Preheat the oven to 400°F. Butter a deep-sided baking dish. Flake the poached cod into a bowl and add the white sauce and parsley. Lightly mix together— you want the fish to stay in large distinctive flakes. Place the bread in a food processor and pulse to make breadcrumbs. Combine with the grated cheese and season the crumb mixture with black pepper.

Whisk the egg whites until stiff. Mix a third into the fish mixture, then gently fold the rest in and spoon the mixture into the prepared baking dish. Scatter the cheesy breadcrumbs over the top. Bake until the top is golden and crisp and the mixture has souffléd up—about 15 to 20 minutes. Serve immediately.

This is a simple rustic dish that is perfect for a winter warmer or a family meal. It can be prepared in advance with minimum fuss and then baked to order. It is very juicy and flavorful and looks fantastic. Cook it in a glass dish and you will be able to see the colored layers of potatoes, leeks cooked with white wine and saffron, and thick chunks of cod (you could use smoked haddock as well). The pie is finished off with a layer of gremolata breadcrumbs that includes chopped garlic, parsley, lemon zest, and crushed hot red pepper flakes, which gives the dish its heat and peppery taste.

layered cod and potato pie
with saffron-cooked leeks

Serves 4 to 6

1lb potatoes, peeled and cut into
　¼in slices
7 tablespoons butter
14oz leeks, cleaned, cut in half, and
　chopped into thin half-moon slices
large pinch of saffron threads
salt and freshly ground black pepper
⅓ cup white wine
juice of ½ lemon
1lb firm white-fleshed cod fillet
2 slices of white bread
2 garlic cloves, finely chopped
3 sprigs of fresh flat-leaf parsley, finely
　chopped
grated zest of 1 lemon
1 pinch of crushed hot red pepper flakes

Preheat the oven to 400°F. Bring a pot of water to a boil, blanch the sliced potatoes for 2 minutes, then drain.

In a separate pan over medium to high heat, melt about one-third of the butter. Add the leeks and saffron threads and season well with salt and black pepper. Lower the heat to medium and cook the leeks for about 10 minutes until softened. Then add the white wine and cook until the liquid is absorbed. Finish the leeks with the lemon juice and set aside to cool.

Meanwhile, cut the fish into slices about the same thickness and diameter as the potatoes. Grease the base and sides of an ovenproof dish with a little butter. Season the fish and potatoes with salt and black pepper. Place half of the potatoes in a single layer on the bottom of the dish. Place half of the fish in another layer on top of the potatoes. Spoon over the cooked saffron leeks, and spread them out. Lay the rest of the fish on top.

Dot the fish layer with the remaining butter and season with plenty of black pepper. Finish the dish with the remaining potatoes, overlapping the slices. Cover with foil and bake in the oven for 15 minutes.

Meanwhile, prepare the breadcrumb topping. Place the bread slices in a food processor with the garlic, parsley, lemon zest, and red pepper flakes. Pulse until you have medium-fine crumbs.

After the pie has been in the oven for 15 minutes, take out the dish, carefully remove the foil, and discard. Baste the potatoes with all the juices from the dish. Scatter the herbed breadcrumbs over the top and return to the oven for another 10 to 12 minutes until the breadcrumbs are golden and aromatic. Serve with vegetables or a simple green or tomato salad.

This is a spectacularly aromatic Vietnamese soup, both rustic and hearty. It's peppery, sweet from the fish and shellfish, sour from the tamarind and lime juice, and salty from the fish sauce and seasoning. In true Vietnamese style, a table salad is placed in the center of the table for each person to garnish their soup. It can consist of fresh dill, mint, cilantro, Thai basil, and shiso or parilla, as well as scallion and lime wedges. This will give the soup a huge amount of perfume and flavor. Any fish can be used, as well as a combination of fish, such as cod fillet with crab or shrimp. Try to find Vietnamese black pepper if you can; it provides a scented, aromatic quality to the dish rather than too much spicy heat.

aromatic black pepper soup

Serves 4 to 6

1 tablespoon oil
2 garlic cloves, finely chopped
5 small golden shallots, finely sliced
2 lemongrass stems, tough outer
   leaves discarded, finely sliced
5 slices of ginger, peeled and cut
   into thin matchsticks
2 medium hot red chiles, seeded and
   finely chopped
4 sprigs of cilantro, stems finely
   chopped
2 quarts simmering fish or chicken
   stock, strained
2 tablespoons tamarind paste, dissolved
   in 5 tablespoons hot water
2 tablespoons orange juice
2 tablespoons fish sauce
5 scallions, trimmed
5 sprigs of fresh mint
small handful of cilantro leaves
30 fresh Thai basil leaves
½ bunch of fresh dill
2 limes, cut into wedges
10½oz cod fillet, cut into ¾in cubes
½ tablespoon freshly ground aromatic
   peppercorns
10½oz MSC-certified white crabmeat
salt and freshly ground black pepper

Heat the oil in a wok. Add the garlic, shallots, lemongrass, and ginger. Cook quickly for 3 to 4 minutes to caramelize the flavors.

Add the red chiles and the chopped cilantro stems. Keep the wok over medium to high heat and move the ingredients around the pan for another 2 to 3 minutes. You want the spices to give off their oils and become aromatic. Pour in the hot stock and simmer gently for 10 minutes.

Add the tamarind liquid, the orange juice, and the fish sauce.

Meanwhile, cut the scallions into 1¼in lengths, then finely shred lengthwise. Place the scallions, herbs, and lime wedges on a platter to serve as a table salad.

When you are nearly ready to serve the soup, add the pieces of fish and the ground aromatic pepper to the wok. Gently simmer for 2 minutes. Be careful that the fish pieces do not break up. After 2 minutes, turn off the heat and add the crabmeat. Allow the fish and shellfish to poach and cook through in the residual heat of the soup. Make sure that you do not overcook the fish, otherwise it will get tough. Season to taste.

Serve the soup accompanied by the table salad. Each guest can garnish the soup at the table, adding some scallions and lime juice, and tearing some of the table herbs into it, before stirring it all in.

This recipe is blindingly simple and completely delicious. What is key is the quality and freshness of ingredients. Use the best heavy cream that you can buy, preferably from your local farmers' market. Choose naturally smoked haddock rather than the stuff that looks like it will glow in the dark. Finnan haddock is haddock split open, brined, and smoked, which comes from Findon, a fishing village in Scotland. Finnan haddocks are quite small, so you will need one fish per person. If Finnan haddock is not available from your fishmonger, get a couple of sides of a larger naturally smoked haddock. This recipe comes from Lady Veronica McLean, who used to own a hotel in Scotland. It is a recipe that has been in my mother's family repertoire for generations. Surprisingly, this dish is not as rich as you'd think, as the smokiness of the fish cuts through the cream. It is a delicious, simple dish, and well worth a try.

smoked haddock baked with cream

Serves 4 to 6

2 bay leaves
sprig of fresh thyme
10 black peppercorns
1 smoked haddock per person,
    weighing about 5lb in total (4 large
    ones or 8 small ones will serve
    8 people)
butter, for greasing
salt and freshly ground black pepper
2 cups good-quality heavy cream

Preheat the oven to 325°F. Bring a pot of water to a boil and add the bay leaves, thyme, and peppercorns. Lower the heat to a light simmer and add the fish. Poach the haddock for 4 minutes. Drain the fish and flake—be careful to remove all the bones and skin.

Butter a large gratin or terracotta dish and arrange the flaked fish over the base. Season the fish with black pepper. Pour over the heavy cream—the fish should be completely covered. Grind a little more black pepper on top. (You can prepare the dish to this stage half a day in advance and set it aside in the fridge to cook later.)

Cook in the low oven for 25 to 28 minutes if the dish is being cooked from cold, but 18 to 20 minutes if the haddock is still hot. It is very important the cream does not boil, otherwise it will split. Serve with mashed potatoes and a green salad.

This is a striking way of making a simple piece of fish absolutely spectacular with a blend of flavors, colors, and textures that stimulate all the senses. The sweet green peas and the crisp pancetta are a delectable combination.

baked fillet of haddock with braised peas and pancetta

Serves 4

8 slices of pancetta or bacon
olive oil
1 garlic clove, finely chopped
1 red chile, seeded and finely chopped
1 medium onion, finely chopped
¼ cup white wine
4 portion-sized pieces of haddock fillet, skin on
salt and freshly ground black pepper
1lb podded peas (frozen peas work perfectly for this dish)
1 lemon
3 sprigs of mint, chopped
⅓ cup Greek yogurt, to serve

Preheat the oven to 400°F. Finely chop half of the pancetta into fine dice. Heat an ovenproof pan over medium to high heat. Add a little olive oil and cook the pancetta for a few minutes until golden brown and beginning to crisp up. Add the garlic and red chile and cook for 1 to 2 minutes until fragrant and aromatic. Add the chopped onion and lower the heat. Cook the onion for 4 to 5 minutes until softened without too much color. When the onion has softened, add the white wine and allow it to simmer for one minute. Remove the pan from the heat. This stage of the dish could be done in advance.

Heat a heavy-bottomed pan over medium to high heat. Pat the fillets dry with paper towels and then season them with some salt and freshly ground black pepper. The pancetta will be salty, so do not over season at this stage. Add a little oil to the pan and place the haddock fillets in the pan skin-side down.

Cook the fish for about 4 minutes until the skin is golden brown and crispy. Do not touch the fish until the edge of the skin is crispy, then carefully turn the fillets over and cook on the flesh side for 1 minute.

Mix the peas into the onion mixture. Place the haddock fillets, crispy skin-side up, in the pan with the peas. Place a slice of pancetta on each piece of fish and place the pan in the oven. Bake for 4 to 5 minutes until the pancetta on the top is crispy.

Remove from the oven and carefully plate the fish. Squeeze the lemon on to the peas and mix together with the chopped mint. Serve the juicy peas alongside with some cool Greek yogurt. A peppery green salad and potatoes (mashed would be good or crushed with some herbs and capers) would be nice with this. Pinot or Viognier would be a good choice of wine to go with the salty pancetta and the freshness of the mint and lemon.

Kedgeree is one of those dishes that can vary enormously. The quality of the haddock is very important; naturally smoked undyed fish must be used, not the stuff that is luminous yellow. I have always liked the combination of flavors and textures of kedgeree, but it was not until I had a really amazing version that I realized what it could be. The name comes from the Hindi *Khicheri,* which is a dish of spiced rice and lentils, and my friend Matthew Rice created a kedgeree that had more links to its original Indian heritage. He used fresh red chile and fresh ginger, as well as cayenne pepper and freshly grated nutmeg. The combination of the smoky flavors of the fish and the spices was excellent, and his kedgeree was often requested and then promptly devoured. The lemon juice highlights all the smoky spicy flavors and makes the dish come completely alive.

kedgeree with fresh and smoked haddock, cayenne pepper, and parsley

Serves 4 to 6

2 cups milk, for poaching
2 bay leaves
½ bunch of fresh flat-leaf parsley, stems coarsely chopped
1 teaspoon black peppercorns
1 naturally smoked haddock fillet, weighing about 1¾lb (or any hot-smoked sustainable fish)
1 fresh haddock fillet, weighing about 1¾lb
2 tablespoons butter
1½in piece of fresh ginger, peeled and finely chopped
1 red chile, seeded and finely chopped
2 garlic cloves, finely chopped
1 onion, finely sliced
½ teaspoon cayenne pepper
½ teaspoon ground turmeric
½ teaspoon ground nutmeg
1 cup basmati rice
2 eggs
2 cups water
salt and freshly ground black pepper
juice of 1 lemon

Preheat the oven to 350°F. Pour the milk into a deep baking dish with the bay leaves, parsley stems, and peppercorns. Place the two haddock fillets flesh-side down in the milk. Cover the baking dish with tin foil and seal the edges. Place the dish in the oven for 20 minutes.

Meanwhile, start cooking the rice. Melt the butter in a deep heavy-bottomed pan over medium to high heat. Add the ginger, chile, and garlic and cook for 2 minutes until fragrant and aromatic. Add the onion and reduce the heat. Cook the onion until softened, about 6 to 8 minutes. Add the dried spices and stir for another minute.

Add the rice and water and bring to a boil. Turn down the heat and allow the rice to simmer for 10 minutes. In a separate pan, cook the eggs in boiling water until hardboiled then refresh in cold water to stop the cooking.

Take the fish out of the oven. Remove the tin foil carefully, as the pan will be full of steam. Wearing a clean pair of rubber gloves, remove the skin and gently flake the fish, removing all the small bones. Reserve the poaching liquid.

Add the flaked haddock to the rice and continue to cook. The rice should be tender but still with a little bite. When cooking, be sure that the rice does not stick to the bottom of the dish. If you need to add any extra liquid, add a little of the fish poaching liquid. Taste the rice and fish and season with salt and pepper to taste. Warm a large serving dish and transfer the rice to the platter.

Shell the hardboiled eggs, cut into quarters, and arrange on the plate. Coarsely chop the parsley leaves and scatter over the top. Squeeze the lemon over the dish and serve to your salivating friends. In a matter of minutes, there may be the odd leaf of parsley or a couple of grains of rice left on a very empty platter.

Like many Vietnamese recipes, this dish is fragrant and perfumed. The fish is grilled or roasted and served in a dish surrounded by clams infused with aromatic peppercorns and star anise. The deliciously scented juice is packed with fresh Vietnamese herbs such as mint, cilantro, and dill.

roasted haddock with fresh vietnamese herbs and clams with aromatic pepper and star anise

Serves 4

1lb clams, cleaned
½ teaspoon mixed aromatic peppercorns
  (white, black, and pink)
1 teaspoon coriander seeds
olive oil
1½in piece of fresh ginger, peeled and cut
  into thin matchsticks
4 star anise
⅓ cup white wine
4 haddock fillets, weighing about
  7oz each, skin on
salt and freshly ground black pepper
1 tablespoon butter, cubed
juice of 1 lime
3 scallions, finely chopped
3 sprigs of cilantro
3 sprigs of fresh mint
3 sprigs of fresh dill

First prepare the clams. Scrub them well, soak them in cold water for about 30 minutes, then drain. Crush the mixed peppercorns and coriander seeds in a pestle and mortar or a spice grinder until they have a little texture.

Heat a little oil in a heavy-bottomed pan over high heat. Add half of the crushed pepper mixture and the slivers of ginger and cook for 1 minute until fragrant and aromatic. Add the clams to the hot pan and stir-fry for 1 minute. Add the star anise and the white wine and cover with a lid. Cook over high heat for 4 minutes until the clams have opened. Remove from the heat. Discard any clams that have not opened and remove two-thirds of the clams from their shells. Strain the liquid through a sieve lined with fine muslin into a bowl. (Clams often have a lot of grit in them.)

Pour the strained liquid into a clean pan; transfer the star anise from the clam pan and add the remaining crushed pepper mixture. Simmer gently to reduce the juice by a third.

While the clams are cooking, roast the fish. Preheat the oven to 400°F. Heat some oil in an ovenproof heavy-bottomed pan over medium to high heat. Season the haddock fillets with salt and black pepper. Add the fish to the pan and cook, skin-side down. Cook for 4 minutes until the skin is golden brown and beginning to crisp. Turn the fish over and transfer the pan to the oven. Bake the fish for 6 to 7 minutes depending on the thickness of the fillets.

When the clam liquid has reduced by a third, whisk in the cubes of butter, one at a time, until the liquid thickens and becomes glossy. Add the lime juice and scallions, then tear the cilantro, mint, and dill into the thickened sauce. Add the clam meat to the sauce.

When the haddock is roasted and the skin is crisp, remove from the oven and position each fillet skin-side up in the center of a large serving plate. Spoon most of the clams, Vietnamese herbs, and juice around the outside of the plate. Add the clams in their shells to the remaining hot sauce and pour them around each piece of fish.

australia
coorong mullet & mulloway

Species: yellow-eyed mullet (*Aldrichetta forsteri*); mulloway
  (*Argyrosomus hololepidotus*); cockle (*Donax deltoides*); golden perch
  (also known as callop) (*Macquaria ambigua*)
Certification: June 2008
Location:the Coorong, Lake Alexandrina, Lake Albert, and the coastal
  waters out to 3 nautical miles
Fishing methods: a wide range of gear types is permitted

australia coorong mullet and mulloway

The Coorong is a rugged fertile saltwater estuarine region in South Australia, where the River Murray reaches the turbulent southern ocean. The shallow salt water was cut off from the ocean thousands of years ago and is now separated from it by over a mile of sand dunes. This wild, wind-lashed stretch of water is about 60 miles long. At its broadest point, the Coorong is 3 miles wide; there are other spots where you could throw a stone across it. The indigenous Ngarrindjeri people were traditionally fishermen and many of the methods employed in the fishery today are similar to theirs. Local fishermen still seek to protect the environment through seasonal rotation of catch and careful selection of fishing methods. The large area of salty water is surrounded by freshwater systems. These include the huge lakes Albert and Alexandrina, which are filled by the Murray when there is fresh flow down the river. This river flow is vital for the Coorong region. Many species rely on it to provide essential nutrients and enable them to spawn, among them the cockles (also known as pipis or surf clams) that are harvested on the beaches. The region is also a breeding and feeding ground for thousands of migratory wading birds. The fishermen enthusiastically participate in annual bird counts. As they operate inside a National Park that includes a Ramsar wetland, they understand that they have an obligation to manage the resource responsibly on behalf of the community. This means not only maintaining the environmental integrity of the region but also enhancing it wherever possible.

Garry Hera-Singh is a third-generation fisherman who was taught the ways of the water by his father and two grandfathers. His family has fished these waters for so long that they are truly part of this wild habitat. "For more than 150 years, fishermen have fished the lower lakes and Coorong," he says. "There have been remarkably few changes over the generations.The methods have stayed the same. It's only some of the materials that have changed. Wooden rowing boats with cotton nets have been upgraded, but that's about it." The fishery is currently made up of 36 licensed family businesses. They are continuing a conservative resource management tradition that has seen the fishery prosper since 1848. The operation is very much community-based, with most of the fishermen living in and around the small country towns of Goolwa, Meningie, Wellington, Murray Bridge, and Kingston.

Yellow-eyed mullet are common all around the south coast. After spawning at sea around Easter, they return to the Coorong and remain there. The shallow, salty water and the food available in this unique ecosystem give the Coorong mullet a special taste. This allows the fish to command high prices. The strength of the fishery over many years has been the ability to move

top right The extraordinary rugged environment of the Coorong is exposed to all the elements that nature can throw at it. In fair weather and foul, its beauty is haunting.

bottom right The golden perch is native to the fresh waters of the lower lakes and Coorong and has been certified by the MSC. The species commands a consistently high price at the Sydney fish markets, and can be steamed, roasted, or grilled whole.

"It is a very hands-on fishery, giving the fishermen an extremely close relationship to the ecosystem, which makes them ideal stewards of the resource."

top left The telltale markings of a Coorong yellow-eyed mullet. On the ocean beaches, juicy cockles are literally dug out of the wet sand with bare feet. When the waves are retreating, diggers such as Linda Alexander and Robert Brooks rotate their feet into the yielding sand and release the pipis. The sweet shellfish are then collected in upright nets.

bottom left Gary Hera-Singh with his handmade rotating fish descaler made by a friend. The delicious mullet were destined for our plates and went from swimming in the Coorong via net and cutting board to griddle pan in less than two hours.

top right Glen Hill says, "The environment is what produces the fish. If you look after the environment, the fish will do the rest for you, for nothing."

between environments and species, providing social, economic, and environmental benefits to the region. The fishermen of the Lakes and Coorong region feel that it is vital to demonstrate to the people of South Australia that they are responsible stewards of their resource. "We put lots of restrictions on ourselves many years ago to make sure that the fishing was sustainable, such as net sizes, other gear regulations, and fishing in time-honored traditions," says Henry Jones, who spent every school vacation fishing with his grandfather. The freshwater golden perch spawn at around 9in long, for example, but the fishermen have put a self-imposed size limit of 13in on them. This gives the perch plenty of time to spawn before they are caught.

A pre-assessment study carried out by Dr. Trevor Ward in 1997 showed the fishery was "inherently sustainable." The families involved then developed and released "Wild Fisheries with a Future," an environmental management plan that was a world first for any fishery. "We went to the WWF to help get certification with the MSC. They were so impressed with the environmental report that they agreed to assist in the funding of the process." After their years of hard work and rigorous documentation, they were awarded international third party certification from the MSC, assisted by the WWF. Glen Hill says that he is "extremely proud that we have worked so closely with the green groups. Along with the WWF, we put together the first environmental memorandum in the world."

Glen and his wife Tracy, who is vice president of the Southern Fishery Association, are trying to make their business as green and sustainable as possible, with a carbon-neutral footprint. They are fishing well under capacity. "We have got the capacity to double what we are harvesting now without putting pressure on the stock," says Glen, "but the environmental cost comes out on a per pound basis." With the fishery ticked off, the couple are now focused on the rest of their business. They re-use all their rainwater and during the six winter months do not use mains

water for fish processing. Their ice is made from rainwater and they are looking at solar energy to provide them with hot water. Impressively, Glen can operate his outboard engine for a week with just 5 gallons of fuel. "We fish to order and after that we stop fishing. That means that all our fish is returned live to the system or used, so there is virtually no wastage or by-catch."

Despite a huge amount of hard work by the Southern Fishery Association and the bounty of international environmental acknowledgement, the Coorong is in deep trouble. The over-allocation of irrigation water along the long course of the Murray means there is no longer fresh water flowing from the mouth of the river. This is transforming the Coorong from an estuarine area into a marine environment. The southern lagoon is now virtually unfishable because it is so saline. Add in the lakes and top end of the lagoon and 95 percent of a system that was vibrant and healthy is now degraded. The current policies are driving the lakes into extinction.

The fishermen of the Coorong feel angry and marginalized. The big picture is out of their hands, while large parts of the system they depend on are becoming as salty as the Dead Sea. They are no longer able to fish for flounder, black bream, and certain other species. Many of the smaller non-consumptive fish that were food for the bigger fish of the Coorong have disappeared from the water. The hardest thing to swallow is the fact that if just 5 percent of the fresh water currently in the Murray Darling system was allowed to reach the ocean, the Coorong region would survive and flourish. That amount of water, which is the difference between life and death for this unique system, is apparently not available at the moment, yet thousands of billions of

above Having a dog in a boat is a matter of choice. Having a wet dog in a boat is something to be avoided whenever possible.

above The nets are put out to dry, watched by the expectant residents of the Coorong, who are never far away from the fisherman and their catch.

gallons of water are being stored for irrigation along the Murray's long course. The Australian Prime Minister Kevin Rudd has visited the environmentally troubled region and promised help, but the fishermen of the Coorong do not know if it will come in time to save this aquatic Eden.

To thank everyone for the country hospitality we had received, we arranged to cook dinner for some friends of the Hills and Hera-Singhs and key figures from the fishing community. The pressure was on and I was planning to cook three dishes based on raw materials that they knew infinitely well. Garry asked how many fish I wanted. I asked for 15 whole mullet for the grilled first course, 15 filleted mullet for the second dish, and some filleted mulloway. Garry cheerily said that he would be back in about an hour. Fishermen tell it how it is and within 60 minutes he returned with everything I had requested. In all my time as a chef, I have never worked in a restaurant where the contents of the menu are fished to order.

As the wind picked up, wine flowed in the fisherman's shack by the Coorong, and the conversation got more boisterous. Fifteen people ranging in age from 10 to 75 were fitted snugly around the table. All eyes were on me and what I was doing with their treasured ocean harvest. At the end of our stay, I received memorable accolades from two of the hardest people to please. Ten-year-old Robert said that he had liked everything, especially the aromatic tea-smoked mullet with a Thai cashew nut, chile, and mint salad. The second comment came from Garry's 75-year-old father Bob. "That was the best piece of mulloway that I have ever eaten," enthused the lifelong Coorong resident. I put it all down to the fresh fish of the day.

The yellow-eyed mullet from the South Australian Coorong region has a unique flavor that lends itself well to many recipes. The tidal flats are saltier than the sea because the water is spread out over a large area and evaporates, concentrating its saltiness. This unique habitat has an effect on the fish; they have a sweet taste and a soft, moist texture and are high in nutritious omega 3. Most of the oil is just under the skin, so quickly hot smoking the fish preserves this precious ingredient.

aromatic smoked mullet with a mint and roasted cashew salad

Serves 4 to 6

1 mullet per person, weighing about
  6 to 9oz, boned and butterflied
2 teaspoons brown sugar
2 tablespoons soy sauce
juice of 1 lime
salt and freshly ground black pepper

For the smoking mix
½ cup dry white Thai rice
2oz jasmine tea
2 lemongrass stems, coarsely chopped
1½in piece of ginger, peeled and cut
  into thin matchsticks
3 tablespoons brown sugar
4 star anise
2 cinnamon sticks
1 tablespoon coriander seeds, crushed

For the cashew salad
1½ cups skinless cashews
2 medium-hot red chiles, seeded and
  finely chopped
juice of 2 limes
2 tablespoons orange juice
2 tablespoons soy sauce
1 tablespoon rice vinegar
1 teaspoon blended sesame oil
1½in piece of ginger, peeled and cut
  into thin matchsticks
4 scallions, finely sliced
4 sprigs of fresh mint
4 sprigs of cilantro

Place the butterflied mullet fillets in a shallow dish. Combine the brown sugar, soy sauce, lime juice, and black pepper and pour over the fish. Line a large wok with 2 layers of tin foil.

Mix together all the smoking ingredients and place in the center of the wok on the foil. Set up a raised rack in the wok, place the filleted fish on top, and cover with a lid. Over medium-high heat, start the caramelization of the smoking mix, then lower the heat and smoke the mullet for 10 to 12 minutes. Turn once while smoking. When the mullet is cooked, remove and leave to cool. Mullet are small fish, so they will not take long to cook. If you are smoking a larger fish, it may take a little longer to smoke and cook.

Preheat the oven to 400°F. Place the cashews on a baking sheet and toast in the oven until golden brown, about 3 to 4 minutes. Do not overcook them, as they become bitter when they are too dark. In a pestle and mortar, pound the chiles with a pinch of salt until you have a smooth paste. Add the lime and orange juices, the soy sauce, vinegar, and sesame oil. Taste the sauce and adjust as necessary; it should be sour, hot, and salty.

When ready to serve, pour half the dressing over the roasted nuts, ginger, and scallions in a bowl and tear in the mint and the cilantro leaves. Pour the remaining dressing over the smoked fillets of fish and serve alongside the salad. The fish will be sweet and scented and will absorb the vibrant taste of the dressing. Serve with a South Australian Riesling; wines from this region have a great citrus acidity balanced with sun-ripened fruit that will enhance the blend of hot, sweet, salty, and sour flavors in the dressing and salad.

Fillets of mullet are perfect served as individual portions, and are easy to cook in a variety of ways. This type of fish can take a variety of seasonings and spices from different cuisines. Here, fillets are grilled or fried and then marinated to take on lots of flavor. If you can get ahold of whole yellow-eyed mullet, then this dish is also great to do with whole fish. Treat them as you would sardines and grill them for a few minutes on each side.

grilled mullet with oregano, garlic, and chile

Serves 4 to 6

½ bunch of fresh oregano or marjoram
   leaves
salt and freshly ground black pepper
pinch of crushed hot red pepper flakes
olive oil
1 mullet per person, butterflied and
   pin-boned (ask your fishmonger
   to do this)

For the marinade
2 garlic cloves
4 tablespoons extra virgin olive oil
1 red chile, seeded and finely chopped
grated zest and juice of 1 lemon
1 tablespoon red wine vinegar

Place half the oregano leaves in a pestle and mortar with a pinch of salt and the red pepper flakes. Crush the leaves to a green pulp. Add enough oil to produce a spreadable paste. Season the mullet on the flesh and skin side with salt and black pepper. Spread some of the green herb paste on to each fish (if using whole mullet, then rub some paste into the cavity of the fish as well).

Make the marinade before you grill the fish, as they take no time to cook. Cut the garlic cloves in half; remove the green central shoot and discard. Finely slice the garlic lengthwise into thin slivers.

Heat a small pan and add 1 tablespoon of the extra virgin olive oil. Add the sliced garlic and cook until pale golden brown, then remove the pan from the heat. With a slotted spoon, remove the garlic slivers and drain on paper towels so that they crisp up into little chips. Do not overcook them in the oil; they will become bitter if too dark.

Add the fresh red chile to the small pan with the remaining extra virgin olive oil, lemon zest and juice, and the red wine vinegar and leave to steep. You are not cooking these ingredients, just allowing them to infuse, as if making tea.

Preheat a griddle pan or broiler so that it is hot. Grill the mullet fillets for 2 minutes on each side and then remove from the pan and arrange in a shallow dish (if using whole fish then cook for 5 to 6 minutes in total). Pour the marinade over the grilled mullet. Scatter the golden-brown flakes of garlic over the top and leave to marinate for at least 10 minutes.

Before serving, coarsely chop the remaining oregano leaves and sprinkle them over the fish. Serve warm, or at room temperature as a starter or an antipasti dish, or as a main meal with salad or vegetable accompaniments.

Mulloway are sweet, juicy, and full of flavor and taste best when cooked simply. They work well when baked whole in the oven. I think there is nothing better, however, than to cook a whole fish in the embers of the fire or on an outdoor grill. The direct heat makes the meaty flesh taste amazing. Fresh herbs, citrus, and chile work together in this recipe to complete the balance of flavors with the sweetness of the fish, although they could also be cooked in Mediterranean or Asian style. If you cannot get ahold of mulloway, you can use another sustainable firm white-fleshed fish.

grilled whole mulloway with basil and lemon dressing

Serves 6

1 mulloway, weighing about 4½lb, scaled and gutted with the head on
olive oil
2 small dried chiles, crushed
2 tablespoons dried oregano
salt and freshly ground black pepper

For the dressing
3 sprigs of fresh flat-leaf parsley
3 sprigs of fresh basil
3 sprigs of fresh mint
grated zest and juice of two lemons
1 fresh red chile, seeded and finely chopped
4 tablespoons extra virgin olive oil

To prepare the fish for grilling, remove all the fins and spines with a heavy-duty pair of kitchen scissors. Be careful not to prick your fingers on the spines. Make two deep cuts from back to belly on a diagonal, following the angle of the head, on both sides of the fish. Rub all over with olive oil inside and outside.

Preheat an outdoor grill, griddle pan, or broiler so that it is very hot; clean and lightly oil the bars of the grill or griddle pan. In a pestle and mortar, grind the dried chiles with the dried oregano and a pinch of salt. Sprinkle this mixture inside the fish, over the skin, and into the deep cuts in the flesh.

To make the dressing, coarsely chop the fresh herbs. Place them in the pestle and mortar and add a pinch of salt, which will work as an abrasive and help break down the herbs. Pound the herbs until you have a smooth green paste. Add the lemon zest and red chile and then the lemon juice and the extra virgin olive oil. Taste the dressing and season with salt and freshly ground black pepper. The fish will be sweet and hot from the chile; the dressing should be sour and hot and slightly salty.

Spoon a little of the green herb dressing over the fish and then place it on the grill. If cooking on a grill with direct heat from underneath, cook on one side for 4 minutes. With a spatula, gently loosen the skin; lift up the fish with a spatula or tongs in each hand and rotate it 45° before replacing it on the grill for another 2 to 3 minutes. You are creating a criss-cross pattern on the fish. Then gently turn the fish over to cook on the other side. The deep slashes will mean that the heat penetrates deep into the flesh, so that the fillet cooks evenly. Repeat the criss-cross pattern on the other side. It may take a few more minutes to cook the fish on each side depending on its thickness.

Transfer the grilled fish to a large platter and serve in the center of the table. Cut pieces off the bone and liberally spoon the green dressing over the top.

I once ate a spectacular fish soup when I was the guest of the Korean Special Consul. It was one of a feast of seafood dishes, including some amazing raw lobster sashimi with spicy chile and sesame dressing to start. When we had eaten our fill of raw fish and shellfish, the remnants were removed to the kitchen where this soup was prepared. The head of the fish made a rich stock while its meat was poached in the broth at the table. It was a very impressive sight, and the taste was delicious and memorable. Soup is very important in Korean cuisine and always forms part of a meal. There is a lot of ritual accompanying the presentation of the soup; it is placed in the center of the table for the guests to help themselves and is traditionally served with rice and many garnishes.

korean spicy soup of mulloway
with scallions and cilantro

Serves 4 to 6

1 mulloway (or another sustainable firm white-fleshed fish), weighing about 2¼ to 3¼lb, gutted, skinned, and filleted (head and bones reserved for the stock)

olive oil, for cooking

1 large piece of fresh ginger, peeled and grated (peelings reserved for the stock)

5 garlic cloves, finely chopped

1 red chile, seeded and finely chopped

2 quarts water

4 sprigs of cilantro with roots

1 tablespoon Sunchang Gochujang red bean paste (Korean spicy bean paste)

1 teaspoon salt

1 teaspoon sugar

20 surf clams, scrubbed

1 red bell pepper, seeded and cut into thin strips

1 small leek (white part only), finely sliced

4 scallions, finely chopped

1 tablespoon soy sauce, plus extra to serve

steamed rice, to serve

lime wedges, to serve

Cut the fish fillets into ½in thick slices and set aside. Heat a little oil in a heavy-bottomed pan and add the ginger peelings, a quarter of the garlic, and chile. Cook over medium heat until fragrant and aromatic, about 2 minutes.

Add the fish head and cleaned bones to the pan, cook for 2 minutes, then add the water and the roots of the cilantro (reserve the leaves for the garnish). Bring to a boil, then simmer for 5 minutes. Skim off any foam that floats to the top with a ladle—you want the stock to be clean, clear, and sweet, not cloudy and bitter. Strain the stock through a sieve, reserving the liquid but discarding the bones.

Wash out the pan and place over medium to high heat. Add the strained stock and bring to a boil. Add the red bean paste, the remaining garlic, and chile and the grated ginger flesh to the stock. Add the salt and sugar and bring to a boil, then turn down the heat so the soup is simmering.

The surf clams are likely to contain some sand. There is nothing worse than a bit of grit in your food, so put a small pan with a splash of water in it over medium heat, add the surf clams, and cover with a lid. Lightly steam the clams until they just begin to open, about 3 minutes. Discard any that do not open. Strain the liquid through a fine piece of muslin placed in a sieve and set aside the juice and clams.

Add the sliced mulloway fillets, red bell pepper, and leek to the stock. Simmer gently for 4 minutes. Just before serving, add the clams and their strained liquid and drop in the scallions to give a bit of bite and texture.

Add the soy sauce and taste the soup. Garnish with the cilantro leaves and serve with steamed rice, the lime wedges, and some extra soy sauce for your guests to help themselves to.

The sweet, rich flavors of a mulloway fillet are enhanced when it is roasted until it forms a crisp golden skin. Here the fillets are crusted with thyme, which gently perfumes the flesh. I use lots of herbs in my cooking and love the taste of a salad packed with fresh flavors; in this recipe, each mouthful will be different—one with more mint, another with parsley, arugula, or basil. This is a lovely summer dish where the mulloway is supported and not overshadowed by the herbs.

roast thyme-crusted mulloway fillet with a warm shallot dressing and mixed herb salad

Serves 4 to 6

For the dressing
3 sprigs of fresh flat-leaf parsley (stems reserved)
2 sprigs of fresh basil (stems reserved)
¼ cup extra virgin olive oil
4 shallots, finely chopped
1 garlic clove, crushed with a pinch of salt
juice of 1 lemon
1 tablespoon red wine vinegar
3 tomatoes, seeded and cut into fine dice, or 20 cherry tomatoes, halved

For the herb salad
3 sprigs of fresh mint
3 sprigs of fresh chervil
yellow central leaves from a head of celery
3½oz wild arugula
3½oz mixed peppery greens, including mizuna and mustard leaves (you could also add some radicchio leaves, chicory, or Belgian endive)

2 tablespoons fresh thyme leaves
4 to 6 portion-sized pieces of mulloway, weighing about 7to 8oz each, skin on
salt and freshly ground black pepper
2 tablespoons olive oil

First make the dressing. Remove the stems of the parsley and basil for the salad. Heat the oil in a small saucepan and add the shallots, garlic, and the herb stems and cook gently without frying. When the oil becomes hot, remove from the heat and allow the ingredients to steep and infuse. Leave the oil to cool for 20 minutes. When the dressing oil is just warm, remove the herb stems and add the lemon juice and vinegar.

Meanwhile, prepare the salad. Fill a large bowl with cold water and add all the herbs and greens to the water. Wash and mix together. Scoop the leaves from the top, allowing any dirt to sink to the bottom. Drain thoroughly, then place the cleaned leaves in a salad spinner and spin until completely dry. Alternatively, dry on paper towels. Place the dry leaves in a salad bowl.

Preheat the oven to 400°F. Heat a large, heavy-bottomed, ovenproof pan over medium to high heat. Coarsely chop the thyme leaves and sprinkle over the fish fillets, then season well with salt and black pepper. Heat the oil in the pan and add the fish, skin-side down. Cook the fish, without moving it, for 4 minutes, then gently turn it over and spoon oil over the uppermost skin before transferring the pan to the oven.

Bake the fish in the hot oven for 6 to 8 minutes or until cooked; the skin will be golden brown and crisp and the flesh will be perfumed with the thyme leaves. Add the chopped tomatoes to the dressing, taste, check the seasoning, and adjust with salt, black pepper, and a little more lemon, if necessary. Remove the fish from the pan and, holding it carefully with an oven mitt, pour in the warm dressing and swirl it around to pick up any of the juices and pieces of thyme.

Arrange the fish skin-side up on a plate. Dress the mixed herb salad with a little of the warm dressing, then spoon the rest around the fish so that the skin stays nice and crisp, arranging a small mound next to the fish. This dish works very well with a bottle of crisp Sauvignon Blanc or Verdelho.

Buying & preparing fish

buying fish

To get the best possible results when buying fish, always try to buy whole fish. If that is not possible, then purchase fish in large fillets (you can ask your fishmonger to cut it into smaller portions for you). Fish keeps much better, for longer, if it is kept in its natural state for as long as possible. With really fresh fish there is a natural sea slime on the skin. This is good and preserves the fish, acting like a protective layer. If you buy fish but are not using it until the next day, leave this protective layer on the fish until you are ready to use it.

Always look for the blue MSC label when buying fish, from a fishmonger or the supermarket, as this guarantees that your fish has been caught in a sustainable manner. If you cannot find any fish with the MSC label, you can ask your fishmonger about where it has come from so that you can make an informed decision about its sustainability.

The fish and the fish counter should not smell fishy. Instead it should smell of the ocean. A fish counter that smells overly fishy with the smell of ammonia is not a good sign.

You can ask your fishmonger to scale and gut your fish for you. If this is not possible, the preparation is easy and not as scary as people think. Four great tools to have if you are getting into cooking fish is a sturdy pair of kitchen scissors, a thin flexible filleting knife, a sharpening steel to keep it sharp, and a pair of long-nosed pliers from a hardware store for the bones.

If you are storing whole fish at home before use, remove the wrapping that the fish has come in from the fishmonger, as this will start to smell first. Place the fish in a shallow dish. Wrap the dish in plastic wrap and place in the coldest part of the fridge. You could also put some ice cubes on top of the plastic wrap to keep the temperature as low as possible.

When choosing your fish there are a few things that you should look for:

- it should have bright glossy eyes, not sunken, tired, and dull.
- the flesh should be bright, shiny, and glossy, not dull and tired. No amount of water can make old fish shiny.
- the flesh should be tight and firm to the touch. If you are not able to touch the fish, then ask the fishmonger to prod the skin side of the flesh for you. The skin should spring back immediately, not leave a sunken thumbprint as on an overripe piece of fruit.
- the gills should be bright red, flushed with blood and look fresh, rather than turgid, bruised brown in color, and broken and old.

cleaning & gutting a fish

To prepare a whole fish start by cutting off all the fins and spines on the fish with a strong pair of kitchen scissors. There are often spines mixed up among the fins along the back of the fish heading down to the tail. Check for any behind the gills, near the tail on the underside of the fish, and near the pectoral fins on the sides of the fish. These spines are very sharp and designed to protect the fish from predators, so it is better to get rid of them to avoid injury.

To scale the fish use a butter knife, which will be less sharp than a kitchen knife (or you can use the back of knife, because you do not want to cut into the flesh). Hold the fish firmly by the tail, with its head down into the sink (alternatively, you could do it outside on a piece of newspaper). Wet the fish with some cold running water. Using a brisk pushing motion with the knife, scrape off the scales moving from tail to head. Rotate the fish around so that you are pulling off all the scales, always working toward the head. Make sure that you scrape right up to where the fins were, along the belly, up to the gill casing, and behind the head to remove all the scales. There is nothing worse than scales on a beautiful piece of cooked fish. It is much easier to scale your fish when it is whole and firm, before you have gutted it.

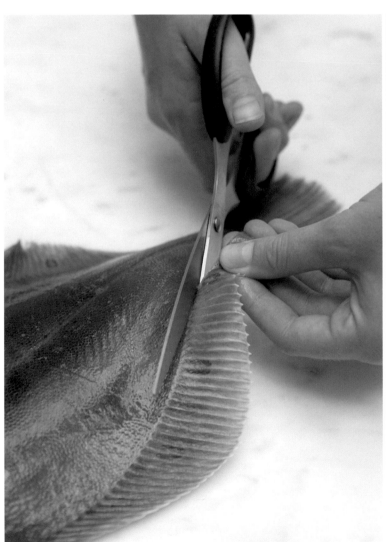
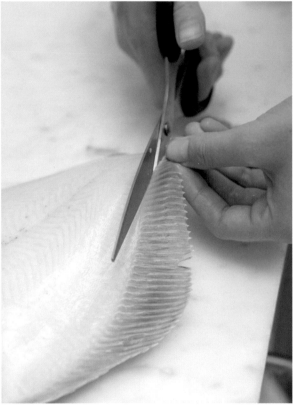

If you are scaling a large fish such as a whole salmon or a big cod, then I would recommend the following: take a garbage bag and cut along one long side with a pair of scissors, then open out the bag. Hold the fish by the tail, as before, with the head of the fish pointing into the sealed corner of the bag. Continue to scale the fish as above and all the scales will be caught by the bag.

Gutting fish is not a big deal done under some cold running water. Insert the blade of a thin sharp knife by the anal fin and cut continuously all the way along the belly to underneath the jaw. You are just cutting through the skin of the belly, so you only need to use the tip of the knife. Use the cold running water to help dislodge the insides. Pull out the guts and cut them free with the knife or scissors near the mouth. To avoid excess cleaning of the sink, pull the insides out into a metal bowl that can get easily emptied. To remove the gills, snip them with the scissors where they are attached to the underside of the jaw. Snip the gills where they attach to the backbone of the fish. Pull out the gills; be careful, as they are quite sharp and spiky, particularly on a large oceanic fish.

Under cold running water, clean out the cavity of the fish. With a teaspoon or the end of knife, scrape clean the dark line of dried blood that runs alongside the spine. Be careful not to tear the flesh of the fish or pull the flesh from the bones.

Make sure that all the blood and gills are removed and the water is running cleanly through the cavity. Pat the whole fish dry with some absorbent paper towels. After preparing fish, always disinfect everything very thoroughly: otherwise, it does not matter how good the dish that you cook is, you will not be very popular.

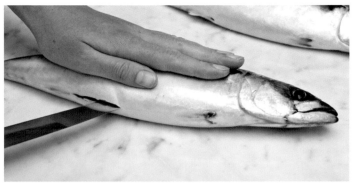

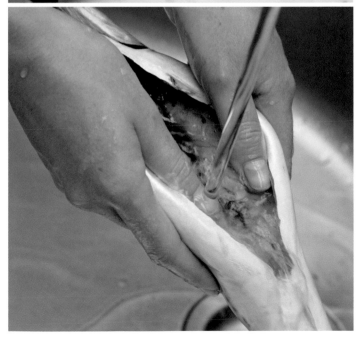

filleting fish

Filleting is a specialist job and at first it may well look like a dog's dinner. Practice, practice, and practice is my only advice. Work on a smaller cheaper fish like a mullet or mackerel at first to get the hang of it. However, it is very satisfying to do it yourself.

ROUND FISH

Place the scaled and gutted fish on the board. Pat the fish dry. The filleting knife that you need to use should be thin bladed, flexible, and nice and sharp. Filleting is so easy and enjoyable with a sharp knife, but hard work and stressful with a blunt one. Following the line behind the head and the gills to the pectoral fins, cut in a diagonal line through the flesh down to the bone. Turn the fish over and repeat on the other side. If it is a larger fish, you may have to chop through the backbone. Looking down at the fish, at the head end there will be a clean diagonal line. With your hand flat on the side of the fish, tilt the fish gently toward the belly exposing the backbone and run the knife horizontally along the backbone, but slightly above the spine, down to the tail. Make the cut in one fluid motion rather than short jagged cuts. Lift the flap of flesh away from the bone like opening a book. With the angle of the knife pointing down to the bone, make another cut, running the underside of the knife along the bone. Repeat with long fluid cuts, with the underside of the knife scraping against the bone, until the fillet is removed from the bone. Turn the fish over and repeat the process, this time running the knife horizontally from the tail to the head.

FLATFISH

Flatfish is much more straightforward to fillet than round fish. Cut a straight line down to the bone from the head to the tail. Make the cut in one fluid motion rather than small jagged cuts. Slide the knife from head to tail along the bones (the angle of the knife should be almost flat) lifting the flap each time so that the knife is scraping along the bone toward the edge of the fish until the fillet is free. Make long fluid slicing motions rather than jagged hacking cuts. Repeat with the other top fillet, and then turn the fish over and cut off the two underside fillets.

FILLETS

To skin a fillet of fish, place the fish skin-side down on the cutting board. Wet your fingers and dip them in some salt to get a good grip. Grasp the fish by the tail end. Cut a little incision with the knife down to the skin. Work the knife from a vertical angle to a horizontal one so that the blade of the knife is flat, pointing away from you toward the head and flat on the skin. In a series of short jerky cuts, move the knife along the skin. With the other hand that is holding the tail end of skin, keep the tension on the skin, pulling it toward the slicing knife. Keep the angle pointing down so that it is not cutting into the flesh.

FLATFISH

To skin a whole Dover sole, place the fish on a cutting board, dark side uppermost. Make a horizontal cut across the tail where the fillets start. Work your fingers under the skin until you are holding a bit of a flap. Sprinkle the tail end with a little salt and hold on tight. Grasp the flap of skin with a kitchen towel. Pull the skin away from the fish right over the head in a fluid, slow tearing motion. Repeat the process on the white underside of the fish. If the skin tears the flesh when you start to pull, then stop, cut the skin around the head, and work in the opposite direction from head to tail.

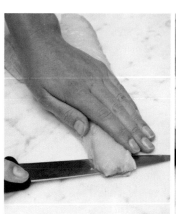   

to prepare clams

Fill a sink with cold water. Vigorously swirl the clams in the water like a washing machine. Repeat with some clean water and swirl until the water is completely clear. Remove any that are broken, do not close when tapped, or smell. Leave to soak in the cold fresh water until you are ready to use them.

Both mussels and clams can be opened raw by inserting the blade of small knife between the shells and twisting the knife to spring open the shells. The knife should not be inserted by the hinge, as when you open oysters, but at the flat edge of the shells. Save all the juice if you are doing this, as it is great if you are making fritters or want to grill the shellfish.

to clean mussels

Wash the mussels thoroughly in cold water, swirling them in the sink as with the clams. With an old knife, scrape off any barnacles that are sticking to them. Scrape the knife toward you like peeling potatoes. The mussels attach themselves to the rocks and each other with fibrous threads called the beard. To debeard the mussels, take hold of the beard and sharply pull upward toward the pointed end of the mussel. Swirl the cleaned mussels in some cold water again to get rid of any grit. Discard any that are broken, that do not close if tapped, or ones that smell; these are already dead and will poison the whole batch if cooked.

Index

Bart's Acknowledgments

Thank you Bernadien for your love, energizing support, patience, and lots of fun during the creation of this book. I love you! A big hug to my fantastic son Bo for his love and all the relaxing soccer moments in between working.

A huge thanks to Kyle Cathie and Martin Fontijn and all their fantastic staff for making our book and my dream come true. Martin, you were a great support during the process. It was a long run but so happy we made it this way! Thank you Vicky Orchard, Judith Hannam, Nicky Collings, Vik Scales, Inge Huijs, Bartina Deighton, and Hennie Franssen for the incredible creation and design.

Tom, it was great working with you. Thank you!

A special thanks to my business partner and friend Jesse Keus with whom I created Fishes. Andrew Bassford, thanks for your business inspiration and non-stop drive.

Many thanks to MSC chief executive Rupert Howes and his staff. Special thanks to Camiel Derichs, Simon Edwards, and John White.

Thank you Jaap van Rijn for your support and great text. Johnny Acton, thanks for helping me formulate my experiences so well. I thank Leonard Fäustle, Chris Arend, Fred Greaves, and Simon Wheeler for the wonderful images. Thank you Reanne Creyghton for your great support with the book.

Special thanks to Stichting DOEN and to David van Brakel and his crew of The Farm Inc. I thank Carel Drijver and the entire staff of WWF and Esther Luiten and the crew of "Stichting De Noordzee."

A specific thanks to Thijs van Banning for his belief in Fishes. Thanks to Mr Kitchen, At van Barneveld, Sophie van der Stap, Sander Emmering, Robert-Jan van Leusen. Thanks to Peter Hamaker and all at Mayonna. Thanks to Ronald and Ninande (Bagels & Beans) and Philippe Vorst (New York Pizza). Thanks Ron Koks of Sligro.

Many thanks to all the sustainable fishermen, fisherwomen, and others involved in the fisheries who contributed to this book: Sylvia Beaudoin; Randy Meier and his staff of R&J Seafoods in Kenai; Jack Schultheis, Maxine and Alfred and all of Kwik'pak Fisheries in Emmonak; Natalie and Jack Webster, all boardmembers and fishermen of AAFA in San Diego; all staff of I&J seafood in Cape Town; Rolf Domstein, Øyvind Reed, John Erik Halvnes, and staff of Domstein in Måløy; Søren Mattesen of Vilsund and Benny Andersen; all people of the Ben Tre Clam fishery in Vietnam; all involved in the Lakes and Cooring fishery in Australia; Louwe de Boer and all staff of the PD147; Paul Joy, Graham Coglen, and all involved in the Hastings CIC fishery.

Thanks to Annelie and René Thuring, Hans van Olphen, Digna Hiel, Vincent and Evi, Berit and Bas, Wijnne, Ivary and Ilan, Raymond, Muriel, Silke, Wilco, Tjeerd and Edsilia, Iwan, Natascha, Levi and Lena, Xander, John, Richard, Martin, and Maurice and their families.

A special thanks to Tom Timmer, whom I had the great pleasure to meet in Newport, but sadly died in a car accident a few days after our day together. I thank him for his contribution to the California chapter, which is of great value to the book and offer my full condolences to his family and all who met this wonderful person.

Tom's Acknowledgments

Thank you Kyle Cathie and Martin Fontijn for this fantastic project. To Bart van Olphen for his creative vision about sustainability. Borra Garson and Emma Hughes at Deborah McKenna Ltd.

Thank you to Leonard Fäustle who has a great eye, took fantastic photographs, and made it all easy and fun. Thank you to Simon Wheeler who is an inspirational photographer and captured the true essence of my food on film. For styling the photographs so beautifully, thank you to Polly Webb-Wilson. Thank you to Vicky Orchard, Judith Hannam, and Suzanna de Jong for their tireless editing, to Nicky Collings for her great design, and to Vik Scales and the fantastic team at Kyle Cathie. To Neal Drinnan, Ed Petrie, and everyone at Simon and Schuster in Australia for their help and support.

Huge appreciation to the people from around the world who so generously helped in the pursuit of this book; Reanne Creyghton of Fishes who made it all possible. From Rolf Domstein and his great team in Norway to Denmark, Holland, Hastings, Vietnam, and to Garry and Christine Hera-Singh and Tracy and Glen Hill in South Australia, thank you for your hospitality and integrity.

To the great cooks who have inspired me, Rose Gray and Ruth Rogers at the River Café, Rick Stein, Lloyd Grossman, Peter Doyle, David Thompson, Theo Randall. To Michael Caines for being a truly extraordinary chef. To Tim Lee and Ashley Huntington for keeping the debate on food wide open and Bernie Plaisted, for being my best man in the kitchen. To the Serious Waders Club. To Heather Patterson Croft and Felicity Jagavkor, who make my life work. Danielle and Rafael Fox Brinner, Kifah Arif JJ Holland, Charlie Mash, Sarah Rowden, Clare Kelly, Celia Brooks Brown, and Michelle Darlington. Thank you Gerald and Sandra Groom.

Thank you to the people who support my career: Chantal Rutherford Brown, The Cutting Edge School of Food and Wine, Books For Cooks, The Essential Ingredient, Susan Pieterse, Tertia Goodwin, Leiths School of Food and Wine, Liz Trigg, Helen Chislet, Jaimin and Amandip Kotecha, Denise Burgess, Hugh, Celina and Gail Arnold, Howard Crump, Alice Hart from Waitrose Food Illustrated, Helen Campbell of Week of Tastes. To Tasting Australia, Mike Chapman at MWC Media. To David Pritchard, Arezoo Farahzad and Grace Kitto at Denhams TV, Amanda Ross and James Winter at Cactus TV, and Melanie Jappy at the BBC thank you for the great projects. Thank you for the opportunities on Ready Steady Cook, Peter Everett and all my fellow chefs, Market Kitchen and Tom Parker Bowles and Matthew Fort and Saturday Kitchen and James Martin. To Debbie Wallen, Annette Peters, Helena Fleming, Caroline Crumby at M&S. To Valli Little, Kylie Walker and everyone at Delicious, Mark Hues at Wine Selectors, Joanna Savill from Good Living, Andrew Boyd. To Susan Foster, Chris and Nick at Favoloso, Caitlin, Luc, and Nicholas Sibulet, Michael Burgess and everyone in Sydney. Thank you to all the chefs and friends who make it so much fun. This book is for you.

Thanks to all within the Fishes team: Jaap van Dijk, Gerrit van As, Jan Kos, Jesse Keus, Jeffrey Prins, Georgy and Philippe Bédier de Prairie, Andrew Bassford, Rolf van Kuijk, Reanne Creyghton, Marc Overeen, Marianne Schut, Yvonne Wickel, Christine Klein, Thierry Abels, Achmed Ait Abid, Noa Ferron, Tonin Vukai, Inge Tichelaar, Clare den Ouden, Jim Schotanus, Eefje van der Ven, Said Benali, Charlotte Oldenbroek, Taco Schreij, Marta Schaverova, Anne Berger, Maartje ter Horst, Marit Lems, Aziza Alhabase, Ron Kievits, Marit Leenstra, Noor Verkooijen, and Michelle Rouwet.